THE GOSPEL THROUGH JONAH'S EYES

THE GOSPEL THROUGH JONAH'S EYES

JON NEIFERT

ACKNOWLEDGEMENTS

I acknowledge those who have helped lead and direct me through the hard work of reviewing, editing, and many suggestions. All of these men are good friends and a great encouragement to me in my life and walk in faith.

Dr. Anthony Silvestro, Jr., fellow evangelist and author, provided useful feedback both on the writing and the content. We had many long phone conversations throughout the time of writing the book.

Al Bandstra, my pastor and theological guide as I learn and grow in my Biblical and Reformed theology and understanding of Scripture.

Tony Ramsek, fellow evangelist and laborer in the harvest, has provided so much encouragement in sharing the Gospel and teaching others through this book. Tony is also one of my board members.

Eddie Roman, fellow evangelist and author, provided good feedback and questions on the content as I shared several drafts along the way.

Seth Roe, my brother-in-law and fellow believer, provided more polish to my writing. I am grateful for his thorough work as my final editor.

The Gospel Through Jonah's Eyes
First Edition

Scripture quotations, unless otherwise noted, are from the English Standard Version: The ESV® Bible (The Holy Bible, English Standard Version®), © 2001 by Crossway, a publishing ministry of Good News Publishers.

Scripture as marked NIV are taken from the New International Version: Holy Bible, New International Version®, NIV® Copyright ©1973, 1978, 1984, 2011 by Biblica, Inc.® Used by permission. All rights reserved worldwide.

Scripture as marked is taken from the King James Version: King James Version, public domain.

Bolding in scripture and other references are mine for emphasis.

The names and pronouns of God, in Trinity, are capitalized to honor Him and to clarify pronouns between God and man. When quoting from other sources, capitalization is retained from the original source.

Paperback ISBN: 979-8-9938192-0-4
eBook ISBN: 979-8-9938192-1-1

Library of Congress Control Number: 2025923907

Published by Tulip Gospel Outreach, 1437 Dubuque Drive, Otley, IA 50214
https://www.tulipgospeloutreach.org

Book design: Robert J. Hewitt III, Livingstones Studio

DEDICATION

I dedicate this book to my family.

To my wife, Verla, who patiently supported me during the writing as I disappeared for hours to write, and who provided practical feedback on my writing.

To my two sons, Colton and Kade, whom I love dearly and desire their continued growth in their faith and love of God.

To our miscarried baby who we have named Sam.

CONTENTS

FOREWORD

I first met Jon one afternoon about 25 years ago while I was on playground duty at Pella Christian Grade School in Pella, Iowa. Being responsible for the safety of the students and not recognizing this neatly dressed man, I approached him to find out who he was and why he was on the playground. He politely informed me he was the father of Colton and Kade and had come to observe them playing and interacting on the playground. Since parents are welcomed to visit school, I welcomed him and we continued to get acquainted. This was the beginning of our friendship which continued to develop as he and his family transferred their membership to the rural Tracy Christian Reformed Church I was pastoring. He appreciated my exegetical preaching and appreciated his stance on a young earth created in six literal days of twenty-four hours.

Jon impressed me then and he continues to impress me. He is an avid evangelist teaching and mentoring individuals and groups in street evangelism at fairs and festivals and actively promoting a historical view of Genesis and calmly answering those who desire to engage him by challenging his Biblical position on Genesis 1-11. God has gripped him with a keen interest and understanding of biblical theology, the wisdom and understanding to defend it, and the desire and motivation to apply it in developing and defining his God-centered worldview.

It was Jon who invited me to join him at a three-day apologetics of Genesis conference put on by the Answers in Genesis organization. Spending five days with Jon was inspiring and invigorating for me. He was as eager to learn more about the reformed faith as I was to learn more about how to defend what I believed concerning Genesis 1-11.

Jon's purpose in writing this book comes from his earnest love for lost souls and his desire for Christ to be revealed to them in Jonah. Luke 24:27 is the foundation on which Jon builds and presents his perspective on Jonah. "And beginning with Moses and all the Prophets, He explained to them what was said in all the Scriptures concerning Himself." This includes Jonah.

I appreciate Jon's Christ-centered perspective throughout the book as he explains how God is revealing Himself in Jesus Christ, the one and only Mediator between God and man. And, as a result of sin, the only revelation of God's grace is in this Mediator. The Old Testament reveals the Mediator who is and was to come. It is not enough to say that God saved HIs people so that Christ might be born of Abraham. Christ is also revealed in every Bible story. All of Scripture is focused on Christ revealing Himself as the Redeemer. His redemption, first announced in the seed in Genesis 3:15, is being progressively revealed to us throughout the stories of the Old Testament, including the story of Jonah.

Jesus did not begin His work in the New Testament, He was already operative throughout the Old Testament. This is one of the reasons God the Father could proclaim at Jesus' baptism, "This is My beloved Son, with Whom I am well pleased." (Matthew 3:27). If we do not understand and proceed from Christ's eager efforts to reveal Himself throughout the Old Testament, we will have a difficult time explaining its stories and history. The acts and motives of the Old Testament characters, including Jonah, can be puzzling and problematic in themselves, will become clear to us when we see the Mediator revealing Himself in and through them.

Teaching and preaching from this perspective is challenging. It's much easier to fall back on our tendency to "find the moral lesson" in each episode recorded in Jonah, making him either a good example to imitate or a bad example to steer clear of. It takes little effort to tell our students that God won't love them if they, like Jonah, become disobedient, but He will love them more and more if they actually live in obedience.

But is this the gospel's message? Is God's love for me based on my behavior? Is it true that if I do something good, God's love for me increases? Is it true that if I do something wrong, His love for me diminishes or is even taken from me? Of course not, He loved us and chose us before the creation of the world, not because we were holy and righteous, but to make us holy and righteous.

The Mediator is revealing Himself in the story of Jonah. Therefore He is the main character and He must be the main character in our understanding and teaching the story of Jonah.

Jon wrote this book for the reader to encounter the Mediator in the life of Jonah. Jon wrote it to help us see and understand the Christ in these stories of Jonah. This book will enable you to understand why Jon is one of God's wonderful gifts to me. I am honored to recommend this book to you.

AL BANDSTRA

A reformed pastor, Christian elementary school teacher, and mentor

THE GOSPEL THROUGH JONAH'S EYES

INTRODUCTION

The story of Jonah is familiar to many who grew up in the church. Many children's books about Jonah and the great fish have been written and illustrated to teach lessons about obedience and God's sovereignty. God knows and sees all—we cannot run or hide from Him. He will pursue you for His purpose, even using incredible means. He pursued Nineveh in His compassion through Jonah, and lavished His mercy upon them. In discipline and correction, Jonah received God's mercy too.

Jonah is described as a prophet; he was compelled to speak God's word as it was given. He eventually descended into the midst of Nineveh with a message from God. They responded in belief and humility and God turned from His wrath and saved them from calamity. Jonah did the work of an evangelist; he brought God's message to the Gentiles, and the entire population of a large city turned to God and was saved. This is the largest revival recorded in the Bible.

Jonah is mentioned just a few times outside the book that bears his name. Despite Jonah's reputation as reluctant or stubborn, Jesus himself mentions Jonah by name. The Pharisees were looking for a sign that Jesus was the Christ, and Jesus told them they would only be given the sign of Jonah. Both Matthew and Luke record Jesus' words and the allusion to Jonah and the people of Nineveh.

As we unpack this story of Jonah, we will uncover illustrations and truths that foreshadow the promised Messiah.

Luke, the author of Acts, wrote of the Old Testament prophets in this way:

And all the prophets who have spoken, from Samuel and those who came after him, also proclaimed these days. (Acts 3:24)

After His resurrection, Jesus walked with His disciples on the road to Emmaus and admonished them to listen to the prophets:

And He said to them, "O foolish ones, and slow of heart to believe all that the prophets have spoken! Was it not necessary that the Christ should suffer these things and enter into His glory?" And beginning with Moses and all the Prophets, He interpreted to them in all the Scriptures the things concerning Himself. (Luke 24:25-27)

Before reading further, take the time to open your Bible, turn to the book of Jonah and read. It is a short, easy read. Keep a bookmark there; you may want to check it or re-read it along the way as we look at the Gospel through Jonah's eyes.

1. WHO WAS JONAH?

Now the word of the Lord came to Jonah the son of
Amittai (Jonah 1:1)

Most of what we know about Jonah, we know from the book bearing his name. What else can we learn about Jonah from the Scripture? He is mentioned in 2 Kings as a prophet in Samaria, the Northern Kingdom of Israel, under King Jeroboam II (793-753 BC).

> *In the fifteenth year of Amaziah the son of Joash, king of Judah, Jeroboam the son of Joash, king of Israel, began to reign in Samaria, and he reigned forty-one years. And he did what was evil in the sight of the Lord. He did not depart from all the sins of Jeroboam the son of Nebat, which he made Israel to sin. He restored the border of Israel from Lebo-hamath as far as the Sea of the Arabah, according to the word of the Lord, the God of Israel, which He spoke by his servant Jonah the son of Amittai, the prophet, who was from Gath-hepher. (2 Kings 14:23-25)*

Samaria had split away from Judah more than a hundred years earlier around 930 BC. Their persistent enemy was Assyria, a country northeast of Israel whose capital was Nineveh. Despite the wickedness of Samaria's king, God chose to restore Israel's border with Assyria during his reign, which He foretold through Jonah.

Assyria was a wicked nation and an enemy of God and God's people. Assyria was one of the earliest empires in the world; their reputation for violence and brutality inspired fear among the surrounding nations.

Assyria was a proud nation with many palaces and gardens. Nineveh was near the city of modern Mosul in northern Iraq. Much of Assyria's military was trained there and their strength was evident in the reliefs on the palace walls. They were known for torturing their captives, smashing people under statues, flaying their captives alive, cutting them up and feeding them as meat for the animals. This torture was a warning to their opponents and the nations surrounding them.

It's easy to understand why Jonah fled from Nineveh, no matter what the message was. They were cruel and his mortal enemy.

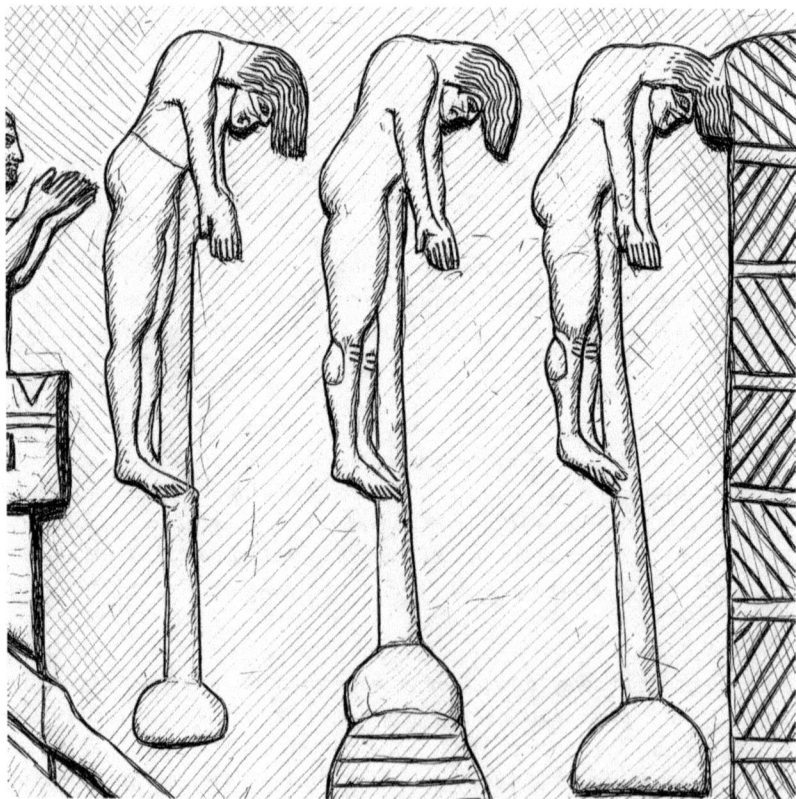

Assyria was infamous for its cruelty, as shown in many reliefs from the palace in Nineveh depicting the impaling and flaying of conquered peoples.

WHAT DID IT MEAN TO BE A PROPHET?

Being a prophet meant a lot in Israel. After God led Israel out of Egypt, God called Moses' brother Aaron and his descendants, the Levites, to be priests. Priests were set apart by God to speak to God on behalf of the people, to offer sacrifices to appease God's anger against their sin, and to serve in the tabernacle.

Then bring near to you Aaron your brother, and his sons with him, from among the people of Israel, to serve me as priests (Exodus 28:1)

A prophet was the counterpart to the priest, speaking to the people on behalf of God. God spoke directly to the prophets, and they spoke to people.

For no prophecy was ever produced by the will of man, but men spoke from God as they were carried along by the Holy Spirit. (2 Peter 1:21)

Hearing and speaking God's message was a heavy burden God's prophet carried. The people were held accountable to God—to listen, believe, and act on God's message—through the prophet. Moses wrote of these responsibilities, even as he wrote of the future Messiah.

"The Lord your God will raise up for you a prophet like me from among you, from your brothers—it is to him you shall listen— just as you desired of the Lord your God at Horeb on the day of the assembly, when you said, 'Let me not hear again the voice of the Lord my God or see this great fire any more, lest I die.' And the Lord said to me, 'They are right in what they have spoken. I will raise up for them a prophet like you from among their brothers. And I will put my words in his mouth, and he shall speak to them all that I command him. (Deuteronomy 18:15-18)

The priesthood was strictly passed through the line of Levi, but the prophet was not restricted in this way. God directly called anyone He chose from among any of the tribes. There were no specific qualifications, training regimens, or examinations by other leaders required. Some were priests, scribes, even simple herdsmen. They generally received no salary; however, in some cases, they were paid to advise the king. We have no record of Jonah getting paid or his profession beyond his role as a prophet.

Prophets had no organizational authority except the call of God. If they abused this authority, they could face death.

But the prophet who presumes to speak a word in my name that I have not commanded him to speak, or who speaks in the name of other gods, that same prophet shall die.' (Deuteronomy 18:20)

God was their authority. When they spoke what God gave them, they had the full backing of God Himself and a mandate from God to speak.

> *And whoever will not listen to my words that he shall speak in my name, I myself will require it of him. (Deuteronomy 18:19)*

BEING A PROPHET WAS NOT EASY

It seems simple: God gives the prophet the words and the prophet speaks to the people. But it wasn't easy.

Israel didn't always want to hear what God had to say. Their desire was to follow the ways of the nations around them, but this displeased God. Jonah would never propose something so vile.

> *"When you come into the land that the Lord your God is giving you, you shall not learn to follow the abominable practices of those nations. There shall not be found among you anyone who burns his son or his daughter as an offering, anyone who practices divination or tells fortunes or interprets omens, or a sorcerer or a charmer or a medium or a necromancer or one who inquires of the dead, for whoever does these things is an abomination to the Lord. And because of these abominations the Lord your God is driving them out before you. You shall be blameless before the Lord your God, for these nations, which you are about to dispossess, listen to fortune-tellers and to diviners. But as for you, the Lord your God has not allowed you to do this. (Deuteronomy 18:9-14)*

The message was not always welcome. Sometimes, prophets were compelled to speak against their leaders. Jeremiah spoke about Israel's sin and impending captivity while false prophets were speaking "peace, peace." John the Baptist, wearing camel's hair and eating locusts, cried out to the Pharisees and Sadducees when they came, *"You brood of vipers! Who warned you to flee from the wrath to come?"* (Matthew 3:7). Later, Herod had John beheaded for calling out Herod's sin.

The title of Prophet wasn't a license to say what was on the prophet's mind–only what God spoke. God established safeguards for the people against false prophets. The test of a true prophet was simple: if the prophecy didn't happen, they were a false prophet.

> *And if you say in your heart, 'How may we know the word that the Lord has not spoken?'— when a prophet speaks in the name of the Lord, if the word does not come to pass or come true, that is a word that the Lord has not spoken; the prophet has spoken it presumptuously. You need not be afraid of him. (Deuteronomy 18:21-22)*

The prophet was bound to be faithful to God's word alone. He was required to fear God more than man and to have the courage to speak the truth no matter the consequence. The prophet Balaam, seemingly a prophet for hire, was urged by the King of Moab to curse Israel.

> *But Balaam answered and said to the servants of Balak, "Though Balak were to give me his house full of silver and gold, I could not go beyond the command of the Lord my God to do less or more. (Numbers 22:18)*

> *Balaam said to Balak, "Behold, I have come to you! Have I now any power of my own to speak anything? The word that God puts in my mouth, that must I speak." (Numbers 22:38)*

> *And Balak said to Balaam, "What have you done to me? I took you to curse my enemies, and behold, you have done nothing but bless them." And he answered and said, "Must I not take care to speak what the Lord puts in my mouth?" (Numbers 23:11-12)*

Despite Balak's desire, Balaam spoke the truth and blessed Israel four times. He was faithful.

The life of a prophet could be lonely. If the prophet brought good news, he was loved by the people. If the news was bad, he was ignored or hated. King Ahab made light of this. After many false prophets advised him to go to war, Jehoshaphat confronted the king about these yes-men and urged him to inquire of the Lord from a true prophet. But Ahab didn't like him.

> *But Jehoshaphat said, "Is there not here another prophet of the Lord of whom we may inquire?" And the king of Israel said to Jehoshaphat, "There is yet one man by whom we may inquire of the Lord, Micaiah the son of Imlah, but I hate him, for he never prophesies good concerning me, but evil." And Jehoshaphat said, "Let not the king say so." (1 Kings 22:7-8)*

Instead of testing the prophets by the truth as God commanded, Israel judged unjustly by listening only to the message they wanted to hear.

JONAH'S MESSAGE WAS DIFFERENT

Most prophets spoke to the people of Israel; Jonah had done that faithfully before. Often, while speaking to Israel, prophets spoke *about* other nations. God called Jonah to do something special–go into Nineveh and speak *directly to* these Gentiles.

We do not know much about Jonah's younger life or why God chose him. We do know that God always prepares each person, according to His will, to fulfill their unique role in His plan.

God knew Jonah and Jonah knew God. Jonah did not ask for this assignment but was pursued by God to reveal His grace and mercy to Nineveh.

GOD HAD A BIGGER PURPOSE FOR JONAH

Beyond his life in the Old Testament, Jesus mentions Jonah in the gospels of Luke and Matthew.

> When the crowds were increasing, he began to say, "This generation is an evil generation. It seeks for a sign, but no sign will be given to it except the sign of Jonah. For as Jonah became a sign to the people of Nineveh, so will the Son of Man be to this generation. (Luke 11:29-30)
>
> The men of Nineveh will rise up at the judgment with this generation and condemn it, for they repented at the preaching of Jonah, and behold, something greater than Jonah is here. (Luke 11:32)

Matthew expands upon this a little more.

> But he answered them, "An evil and adulterous generation seeks for a sign, but no sign will be given to it except the sign of the prophet Jonah. For just as Jonah was three days and three nights in the belly of the great fish, so will the Son of Man be three days and three nights in the heart of the earth. The men of Nineveh will rise up at the judgment with this generation and condemn it, for they repented at the preaching of Jonah, and behold, something greater than Jonah is here. (Matthew 12:39-41)

These passages confirm Jonah as a sign to God's people and an archetype of Christ. Jonah's story serves as a reminder of Jesus' death, burial and resurrection. Studying Jonah reveals many similarities with Christ and the Gospel. Here are a couple of simple examples.

Jesus was from Nazareth. Jonah was from a small village called Gath-hepher, only 2 miles away.

Jonah's name in Hebrew means *dove* and the dove is a symbol of peace or of the Holy Spirit. At the conclusion of The Flood, Noah sent out a dove three times and the third time it did not return. Peace was again upon the earth as the waters of God's wrath subsided. When John baptized Jesus in the Jordan river, a dove served as a symbol of the Holy Spirit.

> *And John bore witness: "I saw the Spirit descend from heaven like a dove, and it remained on him." (John 1:32)*

Jonah brought peace and reconciliation to Nineveh, to those who believed.

> *How beautiful upon the mountains are the feet of him who brings good news, who publishes peace, who brings good news of happiness, who publishes salvation, who says to Zion, "Your God reigns." (Isaiah 52:7)*

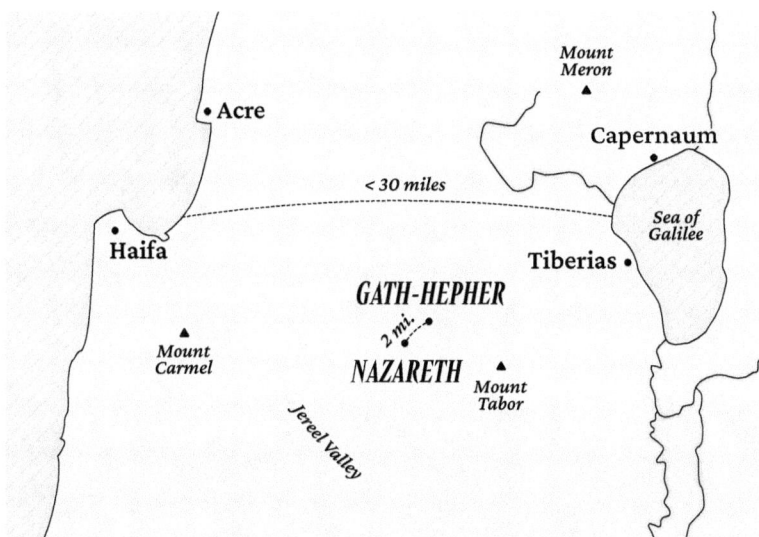

Jonah lived near Nazareth, in the region between the Mediterranean Sea and the Sea of Galilee, a span of less than thirty miles.

2. A PROPHET CALLED BY GOD

"Arise, go to Nineveh, that great city, and call out against
it, for their evil has come up before me." (Jonah 1:2)

As we enter the Biblical story, God calls Jonah to go to Nineveh and preach against it. God had already established Jonah as a prophet, now He directs him to Nineveh. God's call was to Jonah and no one else. It was not transferable. It was a call to action, not just belief. It was a specific call to a faithful prophet: *"go to Nineveh."* God gave him the message directly. Jonah knew God's voice; there was no mistaking His call, just as Christians today know Jesus' voice.

My sheep hear my voice, and I know them, and they follow me. (John 10:27)

Jonah did not want to go; however, he knew God and honored Him by praying to Him, acknowledging God's superiority over his own. In his prayer he complained, but he also praised God for His attributes of grace, mercy, patience, and love. He loved those qualities but did not want God to provide them to Nineveh.

And he prayed to the Lord and said, "O Lord, is not this what I said when I was yet in my country? That is why I made haste to flee to Tarshish; for I knew that you are a gracious God and merciful, slow to anger and abounding in steadfast love, and relenting from disaster. (Jonah 4:2)

Jonah had to do more than just believe, he had to act. God said *"Arise, go to Nineveh."*

He used the same language as He did with Joshua and Philip the Evangelist.

> *After the death of Moses the servant of the Lord, the Lord said to Joshua the son of Nun, Moses' assistant, "Moses my servant is dead. Now therefore **arise, go** over this Jordan, you and all this people, into the land that I am giving to them, to the people of Israel. (Joshua 1:1-2)*

> *Now an angel of the Lord said to Philip, "**Rise and go** toward the south to the road that goes down from Jerusalem to Gaza." This is a desert place. And **he rose and went**. And there was an Ethiopian, a eunuch, a court official of Candace, queen of the Ethiopians, who was in charge of all her treasure. He had come to Jerusalem to worship and was returning, seated in his chariot, and he was reading the prophet Isaiah. And the Spirit said to Philip, "**Go over and join this chariot.**" So Philip ran to him and heard him reading Isaiah the prophet and asked, "Do you understand what you are reading?" (Acts 8:26-30)*

And with many others as well:

> *And the hand of the Lord was upon me there. And he said to me, "**Arise, go** out into the valley, and there I will speak with you." So I arose and went out into the valley, and behold, the glory of the Lord stood there, like the glory that I had seen by the Chebar canal, and I fell on my face. (Ezekiel 3:22-23)*

> *And while Peter was pondering the vision, the Spirit said to him, "Behold, three men are looking for you. **Rise and go** down and accompany them without hesitation, for I have sent them." And Peter went down to the men and said, "I am the one you are looking for. What is the reason for your coming?" (Acts 10:19-21)*

> *And as he entered a village, he was met by ten lepers, who stood at a distance and lifted up their voices, saying, "Jesus, Master, have mercy on us." When he saw them he said to them, "**Go and show** yourselves to the priests." And as they went they were cleansed. (Luke 17:12-14)*

> *Then Jesus answered, "Were not ten cleansed? Where are the nine? Was no one found to return and give praise to God except this foreigner?" And he said to him, "**Rise and go** your way; your faith has made you well." (Luke 17:17-19)*

> *And Jesus came and said to them, "All authority in heaven and on earth has been given to me. **Go** therefore and make disciples of all nations, baptizing them in the name of the Father and of the Son and of the Holy Spirit, teaching them to observe all that*

I have commanded you. And behold, I am with you always, to the end of the age."
(Matthew 28:18-20)

*And he said to them, "**Go into all the world** and proclaim the gospel to the whole cre-*
ation. (Mark 16:15)

*And the master said to the servant, '**Go out to the highways and hedges** and compel*
people to come in, that my house may be filled. (Luke 14:23)

The call to Jonah to go to Nineveh was irrevocable. Jonah tried to run, but God's
call remained. Even after Jonah fled, God repeated His call to Jonah in chapter
3. When God calls, it is easier to just do what He says. He does not relent.

Behold, I received a command to bless: He has blessed, and I cannot revoke it.
(Numbers 23:20)

For the gifts and the calling of God are irrevocable. (Romans 11:29)

GOD'S PURPOSE FOR THE PEOPLE OF NINEVEH?

Whenever God calls, there is a purpose. God may reveal that purpose, or it may
remain a mystery for a time. Jonah was given a general sense of God's purpose
when he first heard from God.

for their evil has come up before me." (Jonah 1:2)

Blinded by his own concerns, Jonah did not see God's purpose until the closing
verses of the book. Here God more fully unveils His compassion and concern
for the least of these in the city of Nineveh.

And should not I pity Nineveh, that great city, in which there are more than 120,000 per-
sons who do not know their right hand from their left, and also much cattle? (Jonah 4:11)

As an archetype for Christ, Jonah's story clearly reveals God's purpose as a
sign for the core of the gospel: Jesus' own death, burial, and resurrection as an
atonement for our sin.

For just as Jonah was three days and three nights in the belly of the great fish, so will the
Son of Man be three days and three nights in the heart of the earth. (Matthew 12:40)

When Jesus invokes Jonah's story in His response to the Pharisees looking for a
sign that He was the Christ, it is clear that God had prepared Jonah for that very

purpose. Just as Jonah could not have known how God would use his story, we may not know His purposes fully until we are united with Him after death.

The greatest purpose of the prophet is to bring glory and honor to Christ and to make Him known. Christ is greater than all the prophets combined. John the Baptist, at the beginning of Jesus' ministry said of Him, *"After me comes a man who ranks before me, because he was before me."* (John 1:30). The Pharisees question Jesus, *"Are you greater than our father Abraham?"* (John 8:53). The woman at the well asked in disbelief, *"Are you greater than our father Jacob?"* (John 4:12). Other passages proclaim that Jesus is greater than the temple (Matthew 12:6), greater than Jonah and Solomon (Matthew 12:41-42, Luke 11:31-32) and greater than Moses (Hebrews 3:3).

There is no greater purpose in this life than to point others to Christ!

THE TIME OF THE OLD TESTAMENT PROPHETS IS COMPLETE

Jonah and the other prophets recorded in the Old Testament spoke infallibly before the people of God. They spoke with authority and insight beyond what man can do himself, because God put His word in their mouths. They proclaimed condemnation and judgment from God, they spoke the truths of God with power and clarity, and they told of future events that God had revealed to them.

No one alive today speaks infallibly, not even the Pope. We are told to test all things. The Bereans were praised for questioning the things that Paul had taught them.

> *Now these Jews were more noble than those in Thessalonica; they received the word with all eagerness, examining the Scriptures daily to see if these things were so. (Acts 17:11)*

Peter was not infallible, and Paul confronted him in his compromise with the circumcision party in Antioch.

> *But when Cephas came to Antioch, I opposed him to his face, because he stood condemned. (Galatians 2:11)*

> *I said to Cephas before them all, "If you, though a Jew, live like a Gentile and not like a Jew, how can you force the Gentiles to live like Jews?" (Galatians 2:14)*

We are not receiving new revelation today. There is nothing additional necessary since the gift of the Scriptures through the prophets of the Old Testament and the apostles of the New Testament.

> *So then you are no longer strangers and aliens, but you are fellow citizens with the saints and members of the household of God, built on the foundation of the apostles and prophets, Christ Jesus himself being the cornerstone, (Ephesians 2:19-20)*

What has been revealed to us is complete; it is sufficient for us—nothing more is needed.

> *All Scripture is breathed out by God and profitable for teaching, for reproof, for correction, and for training in righteousness, that the man of God may be complete, equipped for every good work. (2 Timothy 3:16-17)*

When Jesus told the story of the rich man and Lazarus in heaven, the rich man pleaded with him to send someone to warn his brothers who were still alive. Abraham's response confirmed that the Scripture is sufficient.

> *But Abraham said, 'They have Moses and the Prophets; let them hear them.' (Luke 16:29)*

God's means of revelation to mankind changed to mankind changed in the New Testament when He spoke through His own Son directly. This was recorded by the apostles, who were physical eyewitnesses of Jesus during His ministry and after His resurrection.

> *Long ago, at many times and in many ways, God spoke to our fathers by the prophets, but in these last days he has spoken to us by his Son, whom he appointed the heir of all things, through whom also he created the world. (Hebrews 1:1-2)*

There is One greater than the prophets, and He has revealed Himself to us directly. Returning to the model of Old Testament prophets would be a return to something lesser than God's own Son.

God established the role of prophet in the Old Testament because of the abominable practices of the pagan nations that Israel began to follow. God said, do not seek knowledge through these means, instead I will give you a prophet to reveal what you need to know. Listen to him.

> *You shall be blameless before the Lord your God, for these nations, which you are about to dispossess, listen to fortune-tellers and to diviners. But as for you, the Lord your God has not allowed you to do this. (Deuteronomy 18:13-14)*

When a prophet speaks in the name of the Lord, if the word does not come to pass or come true, that is a word that the Lord has not spoken; the prophet has spoken it presumptuously. You need not be afraid of him. (Deuteronomy 18:22)

Those today who claim to know the future or hear from the Holy Spirit with a new revelation or have a special message from God are speaking presumptuously. While I was witnessing on the street one day, a woman came to me, excited to share that she had heard a message from God that He hadn't told to anyone else. She was speaking presumptuously.

The role of the prophet today does not include speaking infallibly, nor does it include revelation of new truths or future events. It does include speaking boldly the truths of God found in Scripture. It does include the truth heard when a pastor reads God's word and explains it to the flock, or when a father teaches his children from God's word during family worship or devotions. Still, none speak with the infallible authority of God, for that authority is only found in Scripture as revealed through the Old Testament prophets and New Testament apostles.

The prophet's call then, like the evangelist's now, is to faithfully obey God's command—fearing God over man—and boldly proclaim His truth from Scripture.

3. JONAH'S JOURNEY

But Jonah rose to flee to Tarshish from the presence of the Lord.
He went down to Joppa and found a ship going to Tarshish.
So he paid the fare and went down into it, to go with them to
Tarshish, away from the presence of the Lord. (Jonah 1:3)

One key theme in the story of Jonah is his response to God's call. Rather than obeying God, he flees. His physical journey reflects our spiritual journey as God calls us to Himself.

When God called, Jonah fled. This is not the expected response from a prophet. When we examine the response of other prophets, we find that most simply obey. Jonah's rebellion represents a fleshly response. When God told Noah to build an ark, he did it. When God called Moses, he hesitated because of his inability to speak but he obeyed. When Phillip the Evangelist was called to go, he went. But Jonah attempted to flee from God's presence. He demonstrated the natural state of man without God: our sin drives us away from God.

Jonah followed Adam's example and hid from God.

> *And they heard the sound of the Lord God walking in the garden in the cool of the day,*
> *and the man and his wife hid themselves from the presence of the Lord God among the*
> *trees of the garden. (Genesis 3:8)*

Jonah went *"away from the presence of the Lord."* Other translations enhance our understanding: *ran away from the Lord, flee from the Lord, in flight to Tarshish, away from the Lord, from the face of Jehovah, from the presence of Yahweh.* All these point to one thing: Jonah was trying to hide from his responsibility to God.

Even after our second birth, we still battle against the flesh. Our desires in the flesh are contrary to God's desires.

> *For the desires of the flesh are against the Spirit, and the desires of the Spirit are against the flesh, for these are opposed to each other, to keep you from doing the things you want to do. (Galatians 5:17)*

Jonah's rejection was a conscious decision. His spiritual rejection was represented in his physical action of flight. Nineveh was about five hundred miles northeast of Jonah's home in Gath-hepher. Jonah went in the opposite direction, southwest to Joppa, physically separating himself further from Nineveh. Joppa was along the coast of the Mediterranean Sea, and Jonah found a ship headed for Tarshish. After telling his story to the sailors (*mariners*), he bought a ticket and boarded the ship. We often tell our story to rationalize our behavior.

WHY TARSHISH?

Tarshish was as far away as he could go. Although the city no longer exists, today, Tarshish would be located on the southern coast of Spain, roughly 2500 miles from Joppa on the other side of the Mediterranean Sea. The fare would not have been cheap for such a long journey. Jonah proved he was committed to run from God. He likely hoped that God would call someone else to this task since he was so far away. Perhaps, he may have wondered, God would not pursue him at such a great distance.

The unbeliever will frequently go to great lengths and great cost, like Jonah did, to avoid God. The unbeliever finds stepping into a church repugnant and may resist religious conversation about God. They do not want to be confronted by or about God unless they believe they may have an opportunity to mock Him or mock those who believe. They desire to suppress the truth.

> *For the wrath of God is revealed from heaven against all ungodliness and unrighteousness of men, who by their unrighteousness suppress the truth. (Romans 1:18)*

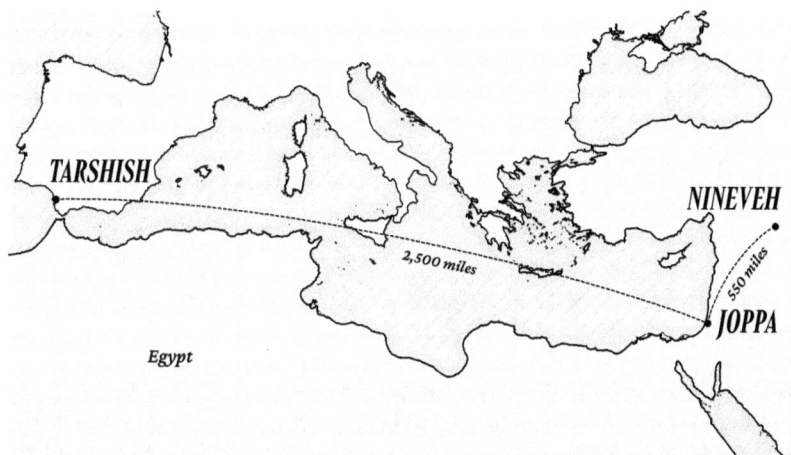

Jonah fled to Joppa which is a full-day drive away from Nineveh and boarded a ship to Tarshish 2500 miles further away. 2500 miles in America would be roughly the distance from Los Angeles to New York City.

JONAH'S ACTIONS

As a prophet, Jonah knew God. He knew he could not really hide since God is present everywhere. He knew God could and would pursue him no matter what or where, and God pursued Jonah in a spectacular way—on the sea through a storm.

> *But the Lord hurled a great wind upon the sea, and there was a mighty tempest on the sea, so that the ship threatened to break up. Then the mariners were afraid, and each cried out to his god. And they hurled the cargo that was in the ship into the sea to lighten it for them. But Jonah had gone down into the inner part of the ship and had lain down and was fast asleep. So the captain came and said to him, "What do you mean, you sleeper? Arise, call out to your god! Perhaps the god will give a thought to us, that we may not perish." (Jonah 1:4-6)*

God is sovereign over all things, even the storms. God sent the wind and the sailors took note. This was no weak storm; it caused much distress for those experienced sailors. They knew to lighten the load, but this was not a run-of-the-mill storm—they couldn't simply adjust and ride it out. It grew stronger and stronger. It struck fear in the hearts of these sailors, to the point that they called out to their so-called gods. God revealed Himself to them through His authority over the seas and storms.

Throughout all of history, knowledge of God, the Creator has existed. He shows His own existence transcendentally to all people, in all nations, throughout all time through His creation—even to unbelievers. God does not allow a claim of ignorance concerning His existence. These sailors, as well as all other people, could not deny His existence.

> For what can be known about God is plain to them, because God has shown it to them. For his invisible attributes, namely, his eternal power and divine nature, have been clearly perceived, ever since the creation of the world, in the things that have been made. So they are without excuse. (Romans 1:19-20)

Knowledge of God is evident from His creation, like the sailors knew the builder of the ship. They knew its quality, its beauty, its accuracy and its operation, all of which reflected the builder. When you appreciate a work of art, you are learning about the artist. When God completed His creation, He declared it *"very good."*

When man rejects the God of scripture, he ends up turning to other gods or idols: we are created to worship. John Calvin wrote, *"The human heart is a perpetual idol factory."* The Israelites fell into idolatry in the wilderness while Moses went up the mountain. They convinced Aaron to make them a golden calf to represent the god that led them out of Egypt (Exodus 32). Throughout their history, God punished Israel for chasing after other gods and worshiping idols. He often punished them by allowing them to be defeated and taken captive by their enemies, including Assyria. There are many such incidents recorded in 1-2 Kings, 1-2 Chronicles, in Isaiah, Jeremiah, and the other prophets. Each time they fell into idolatry, God restored them after a time of discipline, and He always held back a remnant for Himself.

The ship's crew was diverse; they would have sailed to many nations along the Mediterranean Sea. They seemed to hold a pluralistic view, each calling to his own god. Yet, they worked together and showed tolerance for each passenger and crew member. They called on their own gods and asked Jonah to do the same.

Jonah was below deck, sleeping deeply through the storm. They sent the captain down to wake him because their efforts to lighten the load and their cries to their own gods were not doing the trick. The words of the captain exposed the hopelessness of their diversity of gods. There was no certainty nor truth, nothing but blind hope that *maybe* one of the gods *might* be real and save them. There is only uncertainty in diversity; everyone is uncertain in their own way.

While today's culture, media and politics support diversity of belief, there is no true hope apart from the Creator. All other paths lead to the same empty beliefs. They are all worthless, and Jonah proclaims that in his prayer to God.

Those who pay regard to vain idols forsake their hope of steadfast love. (Jonah 2:8)

Diversity and pluralism lead to an exponential growth of ideas. In this type of culture, everyone leaves others to their own belief, because they want to be left to their own beliefs, never arriving at the truth. Diversity will tolerate anything but the exclusivity of the God of Scripture. Acknowledging the God who created them and has authority over them would threaten their pursuit of their own desires. Only the God of the Bible has the power and authority to give assurance and hope. There is, and only can be, one true God. False gods lead to trying to be "good enough," to seeking "happiness or peace," or to appeasing the quest for a "personal god."

Israel strayed and put their hope in Baal during the time of the prophet Elijah. Their idols were worthless and Elijah mocked the four hundred prophets of Baal for calling out to their made up god:

Then Elijah said to the prophets of Baal, "Choose for yourselves one bull and prepare it first, for you are many, and call upon the name of your god, but put no fire to it." And they took the bull that was given them, and they prepared it and called upon the name of Baal from morning until noon, saying, "O Baal, answer us!" But there was no voice, and no one answered. And they limped around the altar that they had made. And at noon Elijah mocked them, saying, "Cry aloud, for he is a god. Either he is musing, or he is relieving himself, or he is on a journey, or perhaps he is asleep and must be awakened." (1 Kings 18:25-27)

WHY SHOULD WE LEAVE OUR NEIGHBOR FLOUNDERING IN HOPELESSNESS?

After their own efforts to lighten the load and call to their gods, the sailors wanted to get to the bottom of things. They wanted a real savior, not an empty hope. They wanted to live and not die. After casting lots, they began to pepper Jonah with questions. They would not accept trite answers.

And they said to one another, "Come, let us cast lots, that we may know on whose account this evil has come upon us." So they cast lots, and the lot fell on Jonah. Then they said to him, "Tell us on whose account this evil has come upon us. What is your occupation?

And where do you come from? What is your country? And of what people are you?"
(Jonah 1:7-8)

Jonah responded in a simple statement, proclaiming his faith in the God of heaven, the Creator God who made the sea and the dry land. Jonah's claim to be a Hebrew was not affirming their belief in a god for each nation, but proclaiming the God who is over all. He confessed God's authority over His Creation, even the sea and the storms. Christians must do the same! Followers of Christ must boldly proclaim the name of the Lord.

> *And he said to them, "I am a Hebrew, and I fear the Lord, the God of heaven, who made the sea and the dry land." Then the men were exceedingly afraid and said to him, "What is this that you have done!" For the men knew that he was fleeing from the presence of the Lord, because he had told them. (Jonah 1:9-10)*

Some believe that we should not speak but simply live godly and holy lives so that others will recognize and desire what we have. However, God makes Himself known to everyone through *what has been made*, and not through our behavior. Others know us by our fruit, but we are not perfect as Christ is. Jonah's actions were not enough for the sailors to come immediately to him for help. They called on their own gods while Jonah spoke the name of the Lord.

When they pressed him *"what shall we do?"* There was an urgency to their question, for they had come face to face with the reality of their situation. We find this same sense of urgency with those who heard Peter's sermon after Jesus' ascension.

> *Now when they heard this they were cut to the heart, and said to Peter and the rest of the apostles, "Brothers, what shall we do?" (Acts 2:37)*

Jonah proclaimed God to the crew and confessed his sin against God.

> *Then they said to him, "What shall we do to you, that the sea may quiet down for us?" For the sea grew more and more tempestuous. (Jonah 1:11)*

Jonah knew God and knew what must be done; he must be hurled into the sea to save the sailors and to show them the real God.

> *He said to them, "Pick me up and hurl me into the sea; then the sea will quiet down for you, for I know it is because of me that this great tempest has come upon you." (Jonah 1:12)*

Jonah did not know what would happen, but he likely narrowed it down to two scenarios. One scenario, building on the most natural consequence for his actions, was that he would drown in the sea and get the death he deserved, his *just* punishment. This would be the righteous judgment of God for fleeing and rejecting Him. We will all face the consequences of our sin.

> *For the wages of sin is death (Romans 6:23)*

The only other scenario was that God would somehow save Jonah by His grace. He did not know how or why, but he knew that he had no hope apart from God. With no other options, Jonah was stripped of any dignity or ability to save himself. He acted in faith, and the sailors and their ship were spared.

THE SAILORS' ACTIONS

Because of Jonah's confession, the sailors feared God but did not want to add guilt by taking Jonah's life. They called out to God (Jonah's God, not their own), pleading with Him to forgive them. They instinctively knew sacrificing Jonah was wrong, for God wrote His law on their hearts.

> *Nevertheless, the men rowed hard to get back to dry land, but they could not, for the sea grew more and more tempestuous against them. Therefore they called out to the Lord, "O Lord, let us not perish for this man's life, and lay not on us innocent blood, for you, O Lord, have done as it pleased you." So they picked up Jonah and hurled him into the sea, and the sea ceased from its raging. Then the men feared the Lord exceedingly, and they offered a sacrifice to the Lord and made vows. (Jonah 1:13-16)*

Once they threw Jonah into the sea, the storm began to calm. They knew their action was the cause of the calm and they feared the Lord.

In the New Testament Jesus demonstrated His authority over the storms. In one story Jesus was below deck and asleep while a storm was raging. The terrified disciples woke Jesus, and He rebuked the storm. The disciples knew no mere man could calm the storm on command.

> *And when he got into the boat, his disciples followed him. And behold, there arose a great storm on the sea, so that the boat was being swamped by the waves; but he was asleep. And they went and woke him, saying, "Save us, Lord; we are perishing." And he said to them, "Why are you afraid, O you of little faith?" Then he rose and rebuked the winds and the sea, and there was a great calm. And the men marveled, saying, "What sort of man is this, that even winds and sea obey him?" (Matthew 8:23-27)*

Jonah did not calm the storm; he is not equal with God. God alone has authority over the storms. Jesus' authority over the storm gave proof to the disciples that He was the Son of God.

WERE THESE MEN SAVED?

This is a question I had never considered before studying the book of Jonah. The focus usually is on Jonah's behavior, the salvation of Nineveh, and on God's compassion and concern for the Ninevites. The way Jonah describes these events and the sailors' reactions, their salvation is a possibility that must be considered. These key points lead me to believe that some turned to God on that day.

1. They saw the futility of their own gods in contrast with God's authority over the storm.

2. The correlation with Jonah's confession and the strength and duration of the storm was striking.

3. Twice it says that they feared God, in verses 10 and 16.

4. They called out to Him in verse 14, recognizing His moral authority and sovereignty.

5. In the end, they offered a sacrifice and made vows to the Lord.

Considering their whole experience, who could hold their tongue? These events were etched into their memory. They could not help but tell others about this God who saved them. However, God opens the eyes of those He chooses; when Jesus healed ten men with leprosy, only one came back to praise God (Luke 17:11-19).

Only God knows these men and their state of salvation. We have no reference to these men like we do the men of Nineveh. God can use our simple testimony and weak presentation of the gospel to proclaim His work before others. He moves people in ways we do not know and often do not recognize.

GOD ALONE BRINGS HOPE TO THIS WORLD.

All of mankind recognizes that there is something wrong in this world as we experience the fear, suffering and uncertainty of life. We either decide to live with it or try to do something about it ourselves. The Bible reveals the uncomfortable truth that we cannot save ourselves. The cause is sin and rebellion against God, it is only in Him that we have hope. It is not our work, but the work of Christ on the cross that brings hope.

In Jonah's situation, he was not silent. When asked, he spoke and proclaimed the name of God to the sailors and gave them hope. We are told to do the same (1 Peter 3:15).

4. IN THE BELLY OF
THE GREAT FISH

*For as Jonah became a sign to the people of Nineveh, so will
the Son of Man be to this generation. (Luke 11:30)*

Jonah's time in the belly of the great fish is the most incredible part of the story for most. It might seem like fiction that a man survived inside a fish for three days, but Jesus refers to Jonah and the men of Nineveh as real people in history.

The closing verse of the first and the second chapters of Jonah are perfect bookends to his time in the belly of the great fish.

> *And the Lord appointed a great fish to swallow up Jonah. And Jonah was in the belly of the fish three days and three nights. (Jonah 1:17)*

> *And the Lord spoke to the fish, and it vomited Jonah out upon the dry land. (Jonah 2:10)*

As an archetype of Christ, Jonah's time in the belly of the fish represents the core of the gospel in Jesus' death, burial and resurrection for our sin. An archetype is never a perfectly complete representation; we should expect to see several similarities but also some differences. For example, Jesus experienced the wrath of God and suffering for us, paying for our sin and reconciling us to God. Jonah also experienced the wrath of God, but in contrast to Jesus' perfection, Jonah's suffering was God's discipline for his own sin and rebellion. Both brought reconciliation through suffering, and both were restored by God.

Between these two verses is Jonah's prayer and description of his experience. He was transformed during this time and praised God by crying out to Him prayer.

OUR DISTORTED PICTURE OF JONAH

The first verse of the second chapter introduces this incredible experience as if it is normal. It's not.

Then Jonah prayed to the Lord his God from the belly of the fish. (Jonah 2:1)

Many of our children's books illustrate this experience in a way that makes it seem less incredible, less horrific. Thinking about Jonah's predicament, what picture comes to mind? We picture Jonah inside a whale (which scripture doesn't say, describing instead a "great fish"). Maybe it's spacious, with a cutaway as we peer into the side of the fish with Jonah sitting, kneeling, or wading in shallow water. Is he protected inside the ribcage with dead fish bones and other debris laying or floating around? Maybe he is sitting on a stool, with a candle while he writes out his prayer? Some illustrations are better than others, but we often do see his distress.

I called out to the Lord, out of my distress (Jonah 2:2)

Several descriptive phrases match his anguish and sense of helplessness as he descends and is trapped inside this fish:

> *"into the deep, into the heart of the seas"*
> *"your waves passed over me"*
> *"waters closed in over me"*
> *"the deep surrounded me"*
> *"weeds were wrapped about my head"*
> *"bars closed upon me forever"*
> *(Jonah 2:3-6)*

Jonah was confused and unable to escape. He was not in a place of God's blessing, but under God's discipline and punishment. David describes God's blessing as broad or spacious:

> *He brought me out into a broad place; he rescued me, because he delighted in me.*
> *(Psalm 18:19)*

Jonah was anywhere but a spacious place of comfort. He was surrounded by the waters of the deep and the billows overpowered him. Inside the fish he was further confined by strong bars or bones; he was wrapped and constricted. It was dark and gloomy, no light to see and no space to move. He struggled even to bring his hands to his face to wipe away the seaweed or debris.

It is a picture of God's discipline. No one enjoys discipline, but we all recognize its benefit; it trains us in righteousness and it transformed Jonah into an obedient servant; a prophet with God's message.

> *It is for discipline that you have to endure. God is treating you as sons. For what son is there whom his father does not discipline? If you are left without discipline, in which all have participated, then you are illegitimate children and not sons. Besides this, we have had earthly fathers who disciplined us and we respected them. Shall we not much more be subject to the Father of spirits and live? For they disciplined us for a short time as it seemed best to them, but he disciplines us for our good, that we may share his holiness. For the moment all discipline seems painful rather than pleasant, but later it yields the peaceful fruit of righteousness to those who have been trained by it. (Hebrews 12:7-11)*

Jonah knew he had sinned. He confessed his transgression before God and the sailors before he was cast overboard. Even after confession, there is still room for discipline. There is also room for grace. Grace comes only after a guilty verdict, for grace without guilt is unnecessary.

Jesus came to earth to die for our sin; this is the Gospel and this was His purpose. He experienced the full wrath of God not because of His sin, but because of ours.

> *Surely he has borne our griefs and carried our sorrows; yet we esteemed him stricken, smitten by God, and afflicted. But he was pierced for our transgressions; he was crushed for our iniquities; upon him was the chastisement that brought us peace, and with his wounds we are healed. All we like sheep have gone astray; we have turned—every one—to his own way; and the Lord has laid on him the iniquity of us all. (Isaiah 53:4-6)*

Jesus knew what was coming and was filled with distress. Before His arrest and crucifixion, He knew He would face suffering under man, but even more so under God. Luke records His prayer in the garden before the final events leading to His death.

> *saying, "Father, if you are willing, remove this cup from me. Nevertheless, not my will, but yours, be done." And there appeared to him an angel from heaven, strengthening him. And being in agony he prayed more earnestly; and his sweat became like great drops of blood falling down to the ground. (Luke 22:42-44)*

Jesus knew what was about to happen, He even warned His disciples from the Scriptures that He must suffer and die before entering His glory.

> *And he began to teach them that the Son of Man must suffer many things and be rejected by the elders and the chief priests and the scribes and be killed, and after three days rise again. (Mark 8:31)*

Jesus endured this agony because it was God's will and would accomplish His purpose to bear our sin, freeing us from the law of sin and death. He became sin for us, and we received His righteousness by grace.

> *For our sake he made him to be sin who knew no sin, so that in him we might become the righteousness of God. (2 Corinthians 5:21)*

JONAH DESCENDS

As Jonah describes his descent, he uses terms describing death and punishment for the wicked. He recognizes his justice at the hand of God.

> *out of the belly of Sheol I cried, and you heard my voice. For you cast me into the deep, into the heart of the seas (Jonah 2:2-3)*

Sheol is the Hebrew word referring to the place of the dead. In a general sense it is the grave; in a more narrow sense, it is used to refer to the place where the wicked are punished.

> *Sheol is found in the Bible sixty-five times. It is translated "the pit" three times, "the grave" thirty-one times, and "hell" thirty-one times. (Berean Bible Society)[1]*

Jonah was thrown into the deep, but who threw Jonah in? He could have pointed to his own confession as the reason, or to the hands of the sailors who threw him in. Instead, he gives credit to God. God had a purpose in this for Jonah.

The deep and the raging waters depict a place of wickedness and of God's wrath. When the waters came at the time of Noah, they came violently. They did not come in a slow, calm rain; rather, scripture says they burst forth and prevailed mightily in God's wrath against the wicked.

---

1.   https://bereanbiblesociety.org/hell-sheol-hades-paradise-and-the-grave

In the six hundredth year of Noah's life, in the second month, on the seventeenth day of the month, on that day all the fountains of the great deep burst forth, and the windows of the heavens were opened. (Genesis 7:11)

And the waters prevailed so mightily on the earth that all the high mountains under the whole heaven were covered. (Genesis 7:19)

The deep was more than just symbolic for Jonah, it had a physical aspect as well. He boarded a ship to cross the Mediterranean Sea. This is a gigantic sea, roughly 2500 miles long and averaging 500 miles across, capable of producing very large waves. Such a vast body was appropriately deep—over 3 miles at its deepest point.

"The Mediterranean Sea, ... occupies an area of approximately 970,000 square miles." (Britannica)[2]

"The Mediterranean Sea has an average depth of 1,500 m (4,900 ft) and the deepest recorded point is 5,109 ± 1 m (16,762 ± 3 ft) in the Calypso Deep in the Ionian Sea." (Wikipedia)[3]

During his descent, Jonah laments that he is driven from God's sight.

Then I said, 'I am driven away from your sight; yet I shall again look upon your holy temple.' (Jonah 2:4)

He was abandoned for a time, no longer experiencing the face of God. Ironically, he had no problem when he fled from God, but when God turned from him, he was devastated.

Jesus expressed the same sentiment on the cross right before He died, quoting from Psalm 22:

And about the ninth hour Jesus cried out with a loud voice, saying, "Eli, Eli, lema sabachthani?" that is, "My God, my God, why have you forsaken me?" (Matthew 27:46)

And Jesus cried out again with a loud voice and yielded up his spirit. (Matthew 27:50)

Jesus and Jonah both experienced separation from God, and both knew they would be restored. In faith, Jonah had confidence that God would not only

---

2.   https://www.britannica.com/place/Mediterranean-Sea
3.   https://en.wikipedia.org/wiki/Mediterranean_Sea

save him from drowning, but God would again restore him. What great joy to be able to glorify and worship God once again, on dry land.

Even in this place of destruction, Jonah had hope. He experienced a taste of God's grace when the fish swallowed him and even more when he was spit up on dry ground.

> *To the roots of the mountains I went down, to the land whose bars closed upon me forever. Yet you brought up my life from the pit, O Lord my God. (Jonah 2:6)*

Jonah was resurrected when he was brought up from the pit—the stomach of the great fish. He was born again, his life was made new, the old self had died off, and Jonah was reconciled to the God he had run from. In fact, God had never fully abandoned him. He pursued him on the sea through the storm and by appointing the great fish to swallow and save him from certain death.

If God could reconcile a rebel like Jonah, He surely could reconcile the wicked people of Nineveh. There is no one we will meet who is too far gone for God to save, to transform, and turn into a true believer in faith.

THE EFFECT OF JONAH'S PRAYER

Jonah began his prayer in distress. His act of prayer proves that he did not abandon God but turned his hope toward Him. And God heard his prayer; it *"came to Him in His holy temple."* This is great assurance, even under God's discipline, that He hears our prayers.

> *The Lord is far from the wicked, but he hears the prayer of the righteous. (Proverbs 15:29)*

God loved Jonah and his temporary rebellion did not eternally separate them. God also heard the cries of those suffering in Nineveh immersed in its evil and violence.

Jonah ended his prayer in praise and thanksgiving.

> *But I with the voice of thanksgiving will sacrifice to you; what I have vowed I will pay. Salvation belongs to the Lord!" (Jonah 2:9)*

Jonah credited God with casting him into the sea and he gave Him credit for his salvation. In earthly terms, there was nothing Jonah could have done to save himself—it took God to save him.

Salvation belongs to the Lord and to the Lord alone. Jonah recalls the sailors each calling on their own worthless idols, even thinking ahead to Nineveh who worshiped other gods. When we put our hope in someone or something outside of God, or in our own efforts, we give up the very thing we need.

Those who pay regard to vain idols forsake their hope of steadfast love. (Jonah 2:8)

Deepening our understanding, the ESV says they *"forsake their hope,"* and the NIV says they *"forfeit the grace that could be theirs;"* other translations say they *"forsake their own mercy."*

Jonah received salvation from the Lord; he received the love and grace required to bring him life. Nineveh received that same grace by the message that God sent through Jonah.

Here are a few simple comparisons showing Jonah as an archetype of Christ.

Jonah	Christ
Jonah was under God's wrath (for his own sin)	Christ was under God's wrath (for man's sin)
Jonah descended into the deep to the pit (Sheol)	Christ descended to the grave (Sheol)
Jonah was banished by God, but restored by Him	Christ was abandoned by God, yet restored by Him
God raised Jonah from the depths of the sea	God raised Christ from the depths of the grave
Christ's work on the cross justified Jonah!	Christ's work on the cross justified us!

Jonah, the Ninevites, and everyone who believes is saved by their faith in Christ, the Son of God. The life of a Christian is a life of thankful obedience because of what Christ did to save us.

5. JONAH'S OBEDIENCE

Then the word of the Lord came to Jonah the second time, saying,
"Arise, go to Nineveh, that great city, and call out against it the
message that I tell you." So Jonah arose and went to Nineveh,
according to the word of the Lord. (Jonah 3:1-3)

Jonah emerged from the deep and out of the great fish–hungry, tired, and disheveled. He still needed to travel 500 miles inland to reach Nineveh. It may have taken him a few weeks if traveling by foot–faster if by camel. He was surely weary when he arrived, but there was more ground to cover as it was a large city.

> *Now Nineveh was an exceedingly great city, three days' journey in breadth. Jonah began*
> *to go into the city, going a day's journey. (Jonah 3:3-4)*

While Jonah was still on the shore, God repeated His command. Jonah was ready to obey for God had extended him grace from his rebellion.

This was not a second chance for Jonah. It was not a new command because he failed the first time. It was the same call. God's call is irrevocable; it never expired or became void. God gave him the same command with the same words. It was clear and certain. Compare these two passages from chapters 1 and 3:

> **"Arise, go to Nineveh, that great city, and call out against it**, *for their evil has come up before me." (Jonah 1:2)*

> **"Arise, go to Nineveh, that great city, and call out against it** *the message that I tell you." (Jonah 3:2)*

Despite his flight, Jonah was restored as God's chosen vessel, a messenger to Nineveh.

PETER'S RESTORATION

Likewise, Peter experienced God's restoration after his failures! In the last weeks of Jesus' life on earth, He told his disciples plainly that He was about to suffer and die. Peter enthusiastically declared his undying devotion to Jesus.

> *"Simon, Simon, behold, Satan demanded to have you, that he might sift you like wheat, but I have prayed for you that your faith may not fail. And when you have turned again, strengthen your brothers." Peter said to him, "Lord, I am ready to go with you both to prison and to death." Jesus said, "I tell you, Peter, the rooster will not crow this day, until you deny three times that you know me." (Luke 22:31-34)*

When the soldiers came to arrest Jesus, Peter, acting boldly on his devotion, cut off the servant's ear with his sword.

> *And one of them struck the servant of the high priest and cut off his right ear. (Luke 22:50)*

After Jesus' arrest, Peter followed but shrunk back, denying Jesus just as he had been warned.

> *Then a servant girl, seeing him as he sat in the light and looking closely at him, said, "This man also was with him." But he denied it, saying, "Woman, I do not know him." And a little later someone else saw him and said, "You also are one of them." But Peter said, "Man, I am not." And after an interval of about an hour still another insisted, saying, "Certainly this man also was with him, for he too is a Galilean." But Peter said, "Man, I do not know what you are talking about." And immediately, while he was still speaking, the rooster crowed. (Luke 22:56-60)*

> *And he went out and wept bitterly. (Luke 22:62)*

Peter was embarrassed, distraught, and horrified, but on the third day that all changed! When the disciples heard the news, Peter was the first to believe and he rushed to see for himself.

> *But on the first day of the week, at early dawn, they went to the tomb, taking the spices they had prepared. And they found the stone rolled away from the tomb, but when they went in they did not find the body of the Lord Jesus. (Luke 24:1-3)*

> *and returning from the tomb they told all these things to the eleven and to all the rest. (Luke 24:9)*

> *but these words seemed to them an idle tale, and they did not believe them. But Peter rose and ran to the tomb; stooping and looking in, he saw the linen cloths by themselves; and he went home marveling at what had happened. (Luke 24:11-12)*

After denying Jesus before, now he rushed in. Peter and Jesus were re-united! He had to wonder, "Would their relationship be the same as it was before?" The story continues in the book of John.

> *When they had finished breakfast, Jesus said to Simon Peter, "Simon, son of John, do you love me more than these?" He said to him, "Yes, Lord; you know that I love you." He said to him, "Feed my lambs." He said to him a second time, "Simon, son of John, do you love me?" He said to him, "Yes, Lord; you know that I love you." He said to him, "Tend my sheep." He said to him the third time, "Simon, son of John, do you love me?" Peter was grieved because he said to him the third time, "Do you love me?" and he said to him, "Lord, you know everything; you know that I love you." Jesus said to him, "Feed my sheep. Truly, truly, I say to you, when you were young, you used to dress yourself and walk wherever you wanted, but when you are old, you will stretch out your hands, and another will dress you and carry you where you do not want to go." (This he said to show by what kind of death he was to glorify God.) And after saying this he said to him, "**Follow me.**" (John 21:15-19)*

Jesus asked Peter three times, "*Do you love Me?*" He followed each affirmation with a command: "*Feed My lambs,*" "*Tend My sheep,*" "*Feed My sheep.*" Jesus' call to Peter was still in effect and reinforced through these words. Jesus knew Peter would fail and yet He planned to restore him; remember His words from Luke 22:32 (*above*). Peter was reconciled to Christ and fully restored to be used by Him.

Jesus' call and command for Peter to be His disciple was the same: "*Follow Me.*"

> *While walking by the Sea of Galilee, he saw two brothers, Simon (who is called Peter) and Andrew his brother, casting a net into the sea, for they were fishermen. And he said*

to them, **"Follow me**, *and I will make you fishers of men." Immediately they left their nets and followed him. (Matthew 4:18-20)*

Despite his weakness, fear, and rebellion, God was determined to use him powerfully for His kingdom.

JONAH'S CALL WASN'T EASY

Jonah's task to bring God's message to Nineveh wasn't easy and it wasn't optional. God wanted him to go into the middle of a large city, filled with his enemies, and speak a message of destruction. One guy, alone! What if they turned and seized him? His friends may have advised against it, but it was God's plan, and God would make it happen with His full support.

The Great Commission is God's command to us today and He gives us the same assurance.

> **Go** *therefore and make disciples of all nations, baptizing them in the name of the Father and of the Son and of the Holy Spirit, teaching them to observe all that I have commanded you. And behold,* **I am with you always**, *to the end of the age." (Matthew 28:19-20)*

It is not the healthy who need a doctor, and it is not the believer who needs to hear the Gospel. We still love to hear it in the same way we like hearing a report of good health. But in God's wisdom our mission field is among His enemies. His enemies are those who chase after other gods or follow worthless idols. They are the ones who love their sin and despise His judgment. The exclusive message of the cross is an offense to the world. It is not us they hate–it is Christ.

> *And this is the judgment: the light has come into the world, and people loved the darkness rather than the light because their works were evil. (John 3:19)*

This is how we once lived. Just as God called Abraham out of his paganism, He now calls the lost out of their rebellion. We win souls from among God's opponents.

> *whoever brings back a sinner from his wandering will save his soul from death and will cover a multitude of sins. (James 5:20)*

Nothing would disqualify Jonah from God's call: not his rebellion, distance, separation, weakness, or lack of desire. Jonah could not escape God's command, and he had confidence to obey because he knew there was nothing that would cause God to abandon him.

> *For I am sure that neither death nor life, nor angels nor rulers, nor things present nor things to come, nor powers, nor height nor depth, nor anything else in all creation, will be able to separate us from the love of God in Christ Jesus our Lord. (Romans 8:38-39)*

In God's wisdom and purpose, He did not give up on Jonah. He will not give up on you.

6. GOD'S MESSAGE TO NINEVEH

Jonah began to go into the city, going a day's journey.
And he called out, "Yet forty days, and Nineveh shall be
overthrown!" (Jonah 3:4)

It wasn't Jonah's message, it was God's. Jonah didn't craft the message and practice it on the way to Nineveh. God revealed it to him.

> *Then the word of the Lord came to Jonah the second time, saying, "Arise, go to Nineveh, that great city, and call out against it **the message that I tell you**." (Jonah 3:2)*

This message, formed directly by God, runs contrary to what many proclaim as the Gospel message today. Our modern sensitivities drive us to tell everyone that God loves them or wants them to have a better life. The false prophets of the Old Testament also wanted to give a positive message because they wanted to be accepted, so they proclaimed peace and success. However, it was not from God; they spoke presumptuously.

When we pursue the Great Commission today, we strive to follow Jonah's example and proclaim the message that God gave us: the Gospel. It's not our message, but God's.

And he said to them, "Go into all the world and proclaim the gospel to the whole creation. (Mark 16:15)

WHAT IS THE GOSPEL MESSAGE?

Some claim that we should just live a good life, preaching the gospel without words. We should all strive to live a life that reflects the Gospel, but we often fail, and a good life by itself has never converted even one soul. At best, our love of others may stir up questions and lead to a conversation about our faith. We still need to use words to proclaim the Gospel. The word Gospel comes from the Greek and simply means good news. News is always spoken or written.

Some have said that the whole Bible is the Gospel message, as it shows God's plan of salvation through all of history. There is great truth in that statement; the Bible is overflowing with good news. It is one giant tract with 66 installments. However, the need is more urgent; we may not have time to explain or show the lost in-depth.

How do we summarize the core of the Gospel? Many Christians struggle to articulate the Gospel because many have never tried, or it is lost in all the busyness of life. This truth can convict us but is easily solved. We can look to Scripture to answer that question and find a few passages that are helpful in summarizing the Gospel.

Some point to the classic passage from John 3:16 that might be seen raised up on a sign in the stands during a ballgame.

> *For God so loved the world, that he gave his only Son, that whoever believes in him should not perish but have eternal life. (John 3:16)*

This single verse focuses on the good news that Jesus came into the world to save but is missing the bad news of our condemnation under God's Law. In the next few verses (18-20) we are reminded of the bad news of God's judgment because our works are evil. It is why we need saving.

> *Whoever believes in him is not condemned, but whoever does not believe is condemned already, because he has not believed in the name of the only Son of God. And this is the judgment: the light has come into the world, and people loved the darkness rather than the light because their works were evil. For everyone who does wicked things hates the light and does not come to the light, lest his works should be exposed. (John 3:18-20)*

This extended passage also points to the exclusive nature of salvation found only in the Son of God, Jesus Christ. We also see the contrast between light and darkness. The whole message of the Gospel contains both bad news and good news. Ray Comfort explains it like this:

> *"no good doctor will give a patient a cure until he is certain that the patient understands the serious nature of his disease." (Living Waters)[1]*

The news of a cure is not understood as good except in the context of the bad news of the disease or illness.

One alternative that I like to use is Ephesians 2 because it emphasizes the bad news that we are all under God's judgment because of our sin. It reminds me, as a Christian, of where I came from and causes me to rejoice that God has saved me.

> *And you were dead in the trespasses and sins in which you once walked, following the course of this world, following the prince of the power of the air, the spirit that is now at work in the sons of disobedience— among whom we all once lived in the passions of our flesh, carrying out the desires of the body and the mind, and were by nature children of wrath, like the rest of mankind. But God, being rich in mercy, because of the great love with which he loved us, even when we were dead in our trespasses, made us alive together with Christ—by grace you have been saved. (Ephesians 2:1-5)*

None of us can claim to be better than the unbeliever whom we are trying to reach with the good news. Sin is the great equalizer of all men and women, for all have sinned and are guilty before God who is Holy and just.

> *For there is no distinction: for all have sinned and fall short of the glory of God, and are justified by his grace as a gift, through the redemption that is in Christ Jesus, (Romans 3:22-24)*

This passage explains that we are saved by God because of His love. Later, God excludes our good works from having any part of our salvation.

> *For by grace you have been saved through faith. And this is not your own doing; it is the gift of God, not a result of works, so that no one may boast. (Ephesians 2:8-9)*

---

1.   https://livingwaters.com/this-may-change-the-way-you-evangelize-forever/

Some point to Romans 10:13, glorifying Christ alone as the One who saves us.

> For "*everyone who calls on the name of the Lord will be saved.*" (Romans 10:13)

This is a proclamation of faith and glorifies Jesus as the Son of God. It points us to the one who can save us but is incomplete without the reason behind it. Without knowledge of sin and death, this phrase might be perceived simply like a "Get out of jail free" card in the game of Monopoly.

The next few verses of Romans 10 help us to understand how an unbeliever comes to faith in Christ. It is encouraging to know that God uses His people to bring the good news to the unbeliever. We remember the people who spoke the Gospel into our own lives. It may have been your parents, a friend, a mentor, or even a stranger.

> How then will they call on him in whom they have not believed? And how are they to believe in him of whom they have never heard? And how are they to hear without someone preaching? And how are they to preach unless they are sent? As it is written, "How beautiful are the feet of those who preach the good news!" But they have not all obeyed the gospel. For Isaiah says, "Lord, who has believed what he has heard from us?" So faith comes from hearing, and hearing through the word of Christ. (Romans 10:14-17)

A passage that many Christians miss is found in 1 Corinthians 15 where Paul directly summarizes the Gospel that is preached.

> Now I would remind you, brothers, of the gospel I preached to you, which you received, in which you stand, and by which you are being saved (1 Corinthians 15:1-2)

It is an anchor passage for the Gospel and connects Jesus to the prophecies of the Messiah.

> For I delivered to you as of first importance what I also received: that Christ died for our sins in accordance with the Scriptures, that he was buried, that he was raised on the third day in accordance with the Scriptures, and that he appeared to Cephas, then to the twelve. (1 Corinthians 15:3-5)

The core of the Gospel is in the work of Christ on the cross, not the works of man. The Gospel we preach must have as its foundation the death, burial, and resurrection of Christ as atonement for our sin. Jesus' death on the cross was considered a curse; He took the curse of our sin on Himself. His death was not the failure of a religious leader, but a fulfillment of prophecy. This is the purpose for which He came; it was a central part of the plan.

But he was pierced for our transgressions; he was crushed for our iniquities; upon him was the chastisement that brought us peace, and with his wounds we are healed. (Isaiah 53:5)

WHAT WAS GOD'S MESSAGE THROUGH JONAH?

Christians often refer to Jonah as a reluctant evangelist because he hid from God before doing the work of an evangelist. The role of an evangelist is to bring the message of God to an unbelieving people. Let us examine Jonah's message considering our understanding of the Gospel. The message was short; scripture only recounts two phrases in Jonah 3:4. We know he spoke these words. If he added anything to it, it would be insignificant since it is not recorded anywhere in Scripture.

And he called out, "Yet forty days, and Nineveh shall be overthrown!" (Jonah 3:4)

It was a message of judgment – *"Nineveh shall be overthrown!"* (Jonah 3:4)

Was this a message of hate? Some define hate as an action taken against a person or group based on bias, such as that found in racism. Was Jonah's message one based on bias? No, because it wasn't Jonah's message, it was God's. Sometimes hate shows up as a stereotype, rather than from knowledge of the individual. God knows all, sees all, hears all. He is perfect and holy and He cannot make a blind judgment.

God sent His message because He heard the cries of those distressed by the violence around them. Do not underestimate the impact of living constantly in a hostile and violent culture.

for their evil has come up before me." (Jonah 1:2)

God's purpose was not to tell the wicked how much He loved them, but to provide relief for those living under their wickedness. The violence of the Assyrian Empire was well-known both in Nineveh and the surrounding nations. In their blindness, they did not see a problem; they probably found their behavior very useful as they conquered nations and imposed their values upon them. However, those values were against God's values, so God pressed them to change.

In God's perfect knowledge and wisdom, He declared them guilty and announced their judgment. This is the bad news: punishment is due and is coming soon. God needed them to repent and turn from their ways. Knowing the end of the story, it is clear how His message caused them to repent and turn to God.

It was an urgent message of mercy – *"Yet forty days"* (Jonah 3:4)

God's judgment is just. He would have been right if He had chosen to destroy them that same day, rather than giving them time to consider their situation and act. It is easy for us to overlook God's patience, but Jonah did not. God gave them time to respond, but it was limited, there was a sense of urgency.

> *for I knew that you are a gracious God and merciful, slow to anger and abounding in steadfast love, and relenting from disaster. (Jonah 4:2)*

Let me use an analogy to further explain. When driving through the countryside there are signs that warn about what lies ahead: "Stop Ahead," "Lane Ends," and "Slippery When Wet" are great examples. These signs give us time to prepare and to take action to adjust our speed for the changes along the way. If you fail to slow down, you may get caught in a speed trap or fail to navigate a sharp corner and cause harm to yourself or your vehicle. It could be worse if it causes harm to another, and you would be held responsible. These warnings are for our benefit.

God's patience and mercy are ever-present; they demonstrate His love and lead us to right action.

> *Or do you presume on the riches of his kindness and forbearance and patience, not knowing that God's kindness is meant to lead you to repentance? (Romans 2:4)*

God was merciful to send Jonah with this warning! It was their sign, and they responded.

Today's Gospel call to repent and believe is a merciful message to our culture.

We can see the same mercy and warning from God in His request to Pharaoh to *"Let my people go."* Through Moses and Aaron, He gave Pharaoh time and opportunity to obey after each of the ten plagues. But Pharaoh was proud and rejected them one by one. Pharaoh could have ended it at any point, but he remained in his rebellion against God.

The people of Nineveh knew their guilt, and God's message warned them that punishment was coming soon. God is righteous and just, and Nineveh was wicked. No one on earth had the authority or power to bring them to account except for God. All men are judged by God and His standard, rather than our own. Jonah was simply the messenger who brought the sign of warning from God.

ONLY GOD CAN JUDGE ME

Unbelievers object, "you can't judge me, only God can!" They are right in one sense. Nineveh was judged by God, not by Jonah. It was God's word, God's standard, God's Law, and God's message that judged them. They sinned against God and His law. Jonah spoke, but the message and the judgment was God's. When we proclaim the call of the Gospel using God's word, it is not our message, but God's through us. Yet, the wicked wrongly perceive this as our judgment and oppose the Christian for judging them.

The Bible does not tell us that we cannot judge, as many claim, using this popular verse from Matthew.

> *Judge not, that you be not judged. (Matthew 7:1)*

This passage does not universally condemn the practice of judgment by the believer but condemns self-righteous judgment.

> *You hypocrite, first take the log out of your own eye, and then you will see clearly to take the speck out of your brother's eye. (Matthew 7:5)*

Instead of a blanket condemnation, it gives a clear example of an unrighteous judgment. God desires for us to judge rightly, not rashly, with partial knowledge, or showing favoritism based on appearances or other factors.

> *My brothers, show no partiality as you hold the faith in our Lord Jesus Christ, the Lord of glory. (James 2:1)*

> *Do not judge by appearances, but judge with right judgment." (John 7:24)*

We are commanded to extend grace and truth to one another as God does for us. For many Christians, our tendency is to be more gracious and tone down our message. However, we must take care when we speak; we are not to speak more harshly nor more mercifully than God regarding a sinner's situation. Jonah was a prophet and compelled to speak what God spoke no matter how he may have desired to change the message.

One additional challenge is that the word "judge" has several meanings. We need to be clear about how we use the word and understand how others may use it differently. Consider the following sentences. I may not judge (condemn) a man for sleeping with another man's wife, but I can judge (discern) that his actions are against God's law. I should hold up God's law, *"You shall not commit adultery"* (Exodus 20:14), allowing him to see his own guilt in God's eyes. In this action, he judges (finds guilt in) himself as his guilt is reflected in God's standard.

Those not familiar with the "*Good Person Test*," should take some time to watch the short video at https://www.needGod.com. This is a very simple approach to share the Gospel, asking the person if they have followed each of God's laws so they can see themselves through God's eyes. It is a gentle appeal to the conscience, helping the lost to understand the bad news before revealing the good news of what Christ has done.

The Gospel is an offense to the unbeliever, because God's Law is contrary to the desires of the carnal man.

> *But I say, walk by the Spirit, and you will not gratify the desires of the flesh. For the desires of the flesh are against the Spirit, and the desires of the Spirit are against the flesh, for these are opposed to each other, to keep you from doing the things you want to do. (Galatians 5:16-17)*

Our actions and our tone should avoid bringing more offense than what is already present in the Gospel.

JONAH'S MESSAGE TO NINEVEH

As we speak against the wickedness and violence in our own culture, we must put Christ first. But our tendency is to proclaim peace and love, like the false prophets did. This demonstrates that we fear man more than we fear God.

> *Have no fear of them, nor be troubled, but in your hearts honor Christ the Lord as holy, always being prepared to make a defense to anyone who asks you for a reason for the hope that is in you; yet do it with gentleness and respect, having a good conscience, so that, when you are slandered, those who revile your good behavior in Christ may be put to shame. (1 Peter 3:14-16)*

We must speak boldly and clearly, putting Christ first: His name, His truth, and His love. These biblical principles require us to point out sin and wickedness according to God's standards, not our own. The way we do this must also be filled with gentleness and respect. We are told to "*speak the truth in love.*" (Ephesians 4:15); and when a brother sins, we should "*restore him in a spirit of gentleness.*" (Galatians 6:1)

As Christians, we are ambassadors for Christ among our enemies. A good ambassador speaks truthfully and with respect. We have a difficult message, but it is necessary. Most parents know how to communicate difficult truths with their children; leaders learn to influence others through difficult decisions or rough waters. Those listening can sense a loving tone even when we deliver bad news when we have a genuine concern for them.

OUR CALL TO PROCLAIM THE GOSPEL

The Great Commission, found in three of the Gospels, gives us the same responsibility Jonah had: to bring the Gospel to God's enemies and make disciples of all nations.

> *Go therefore and make disciples of all nations, baptizing them in the name of the Father and of the Son and of the Holy Spirit, teaching them to observe all that I have commanded you. And behold, I am with you always, to the end of the age." (Matthew 28:19-20)*

> *And he said to them, "Go into all the world and proclaim the gospel to the whole creation. (Mark 16:15)*

> *and said to them, "Thus it is written, that the Christ should suffer and on the third day rise from the dead, and that repentance for the forgiveness of sins should be proclaimed in his name to all nations, beginning from Jerusalem. (Luke 24:46-47)*

We have the same command as Jonah: to bring God's message to His people. We have God's message–the Gospel as found in His Word.

The scope of God's commission for Jonah was the city of Nineveh. Jonah was faithful in bringing God's message to the people of Nineveh. He went through the whole city continuing to herald the message that God gave him. Jonah 3:4 says he went *"a day's journey"* and Jonah 4:5 shows he went completely through, coming out on the opposite side. He journeyed from the west, coming from the Mediterranean Sea, and ended up outside the city on the east side.

> *Jonah went out of the city and sat to the east of the city and made a booth for himself there (Jonah 4:5)*

Jonah did not short-change God in completing his vow. He proclaimed the whole message to the whole city, just as God had given it to him.

The greatest message we can give is God's message. Jonah used God's words to bring His message to Nineveh. There was no human reason for anyone to listen to Jonah. The words we speak carry the wisdom and authority of their source. Our words are opinion–God's words are truth.

7. NINEVEH RESPONDS

And the people of Nineveh believed God. They called for a
fast and put on sackcloth, from the greatest of them to the
least of them. (Jonah 3:5)

Jonah proclaimed God's message, and the people responded correctly. What joy that should have given to Jonah and every believer. Instead, Jonah became angry with God in his own desire to see the destruction of Nineveh. First, let us examine how Nineveh responded.

NINEVEH RESPONDED IN FAITH

Five verses in the middle of chapter 3 tell us the impact of the message on the people of Nineveh. We will examine these step by step, but their starting point is central to the Gospel even today.

And the people of Nineveh believed God. (Jonah 3:5)

The first thing mentioned is belief; they were saved by faith and not by works!

Salvation, even in the Old Testament, was by faith. Faith was the only means of salvation before Christ came, even before Martin Luther challenged the Roman Catholic Church on this point during the Reformation. Salvation has always been by God, through faith in Him. Hebrews 11 tells how the forefathers of Israel acted in faith. Our faith is first and foremost, then out of faith our actions proceed.

> *Now faith is the assurance of things hoped for, the conviction of things not seen. For by it the people of old received their commendation. (Hebrews 11:1-2)*

Abraham was saved by faith in God from the very beginning. God called him out of his pagan religion and its practices, away from his family and country.

> *Now the LORD said to Abram, "Go from your country and your kindred and your father's house to the land that I will show you (Genesis 12:1)*

> *And he brought him outside and said, "Look toward heaven, and number the stars, if you are able to number them." Then he said to him, "So shall your offspring be." And **he believed the Lord**, and He counted it to him as righteousness. (Genesis 15:5-6)*

James references this as well.

> *and the Scripture was fulfilled that says, "Abraham believed God, and it was counted to him as righteousness"—and he was called a friend of God. (James 2:23)*

Martin Luther struggled with the works-based system as he studied in the monastery in the sixteenth century. Eventually, his conscience could bear no more, and he was compelled by the thought that his works would never be enough. Instead, the Lord opened his eyes to understand the truth summarized in Romans 1.

> *For I am not ashamed of the gospel, for it is the power of God for salvation to everyone who believes, to the Jew first and also to the Greek. For in it the righteousness of God is revealed from faith for faith, as it is written, "The righteous shall live by faith. (Romans 1:16-17)*

Salvation comes by grace, through faith in Christ by the message of the Gospel to the whole world, not only to the Jew, but also to the Gentile. This is more clearly taught in the New Testament, but Jonah's mission trip to Nineveh demonstrated this truth to the people of his generation. Men of the Old Testament were saved by faith in one God and His promise of salvation through the Messiah who would bear their transgressions.

In contrast, the rebellious man believes that he is saved by doing good things, avoiding harm to others, or by his devotion to appease God's anger. But his actions are unable to save him; he can only be saved by Christ's grace, given on the cross and paid in His blood, through faith.

If with Christ you died to the elemental spirits of the world, why, as if you were still alive in the world, do you submit to regulations— "Do not handle, Do not taste, Do not touch" (referring to things that all perish as they are used)—according to human precepts and teachings? These have indeed an appearance of wisdom in promoting self-made religion and asceticism and severity to the body, but they are of no value in stopping the indulgence of the flesh. (Colossians 2:20-23)

Our pride drives us to convince ourselves that we can be good enough to deserve God's acceptance.

NINEVEH RESPONDED IN HUMILITY

The men of Nineveh had much reason for pride; they conquered many people and nations through their strength. Instead of leaning on their own strength to run Jonah out of town, they responded in faith and humbled themselves. This response rippled across the whole city as the message reached each one.

They called for a fast and put on sackcloth, from the greatest of them to the least of them. (Jonah 3:5)

The alternative to pride is a humble faith. A proud faith still acts in pride, lording it over others to do the same. A proud faith boasts in how wise or diligent or privileged one is to understand and believe the message. It boasts, even if silently, elevating self. A humble faith elevates God rather than self. Habakkuk warns against this as he reminds us that we live by faith.

Behold, his soul is puffed up; it is not upright within him, but the righteous shall live by his faith. (Habakkuk 2:4)

This is echoed by Paul in his letter to the Ephesians. Righteousness is not the result of anything we do or say. God alone saves as Jonah recognized in his prayer from the great fish.

For by grace you have been saved through faith. And this is not your own doing; it is the gift of God, not a result of works, so that no one may boast. (Ephesians 2:8-9)

Many verses confirm our salvation through faith, by God's work and not our own. Jonah acknowledged that in his prayer, *"Salvation belongs to the LORD!"*

Now it is evident that no one is justified before God by the law, for "The righteous shall live by faith. (Galatians 3:11)

And God, who knows the heart, bore witness to them, by giving them the Holy Spirit just as he did to us, and he made no distinction between us and them, having cleansed their hearts by faith. (Acts 15:8-9)

Salvation by faith puts us on equal ground with all others rather than elevating us in pride. A man's station in life is irrelevant; even the king of Nineveh humbled himself, setting aside his robe as the symbol of his power and authority and physically sat in ashes and sackcloth.

The word reached the king of Nineveh, and he arose from his throne, removed his robe, covered himself with sackcloth, and sat in ashes. (Jonah 3:6)

Nineveh's response to God's message started with the people; Jonah had gone only one-day's journey into the city before appealing to the people that God put in his path.

NINEVEH REPENTED

God's purpose and intent was for Nineveh to repent, and to provide relief for those who had cried out to Him in their distress. Their evil ways required a change that God accomplished through His message. The king repented and used his authority to urge the citizens to respond as he did and as he commanded.

And he issued a proclamation and published through Nineveh, "By the decree of the king and his nobles: Let neither man nor beast, herd nor flock, taste anything. Let them not feed or drink water, but let man and beast be covered with sackcloth, and let them call out mightily to God. Let everyone turn from his evil way and from the violence that is in his hands. (Jonah 3:7-8)

He called on everyone to repent, to "*turn from his evil way and from the violence that is in his hands.*" The king and the people knew they were acting in wickedness, and their response demonstrated their newly professed faith. They knew this because God's Law was written on their hearts, every one of them. Their faith was more than just a verbal claim; they put their faith into action.

James challenges us to evaluate our own faith: is it a faith that saves or is it just an empty claim? Doing what God commands is the evidence of faith.

What good is it, my brothers, if someone says he has faith but does not have works? Can that faith save him? (James 2:14)

For as the body apart from the spirit is dead, so also faith apart from works is dead. (James 2:26)

Mankind has a deceptive nature, seeking to put on a good front for others to see. We say, "Listen to what I say, not what I do." Our behavior reveals to others who we are and what we believe. As a general principle, our actions follow our belief. To act contrary to what you truly believe is unnatural and unsustainable. Eventually, the truth comes out in our actions, or through our words.

for out of the abundance of the heart his mouth speaks. (Luke 6:45)

NINEVEH REJECTED THEIR OWN GODS

Recall that during Jonah's time on the ship in the midst of the storm, the sailors called out, each to their own god. Their captain urged Jonah to do the same. In Nineveh, in the king's proclamation he appeals to God, the God of Israel. In doing so, he abandoned his own gods that he and the whole city had worshiped and put their trust in.

Who knows? God may turn and relent and turn from his fierce anger, so that we may not perish." (Jonah 3:9)

Throughout their history, Nineveh and the people of Assyria had served other gods, including Ishtar, the fertility goddess, and Dagon, the fish-god. They built temples and monuments to honor and worship these false gods and engage in their wicked practices. They were now at the mercy of the one true God, the Creator and Sovereign of the universe. The Gospel calls us to an exclusive claim of one God, and one Redeemer.

This Jesus is the stone that was rejected by you, the builders, which has become the cornerstone. And there is salvation in no one else, for there is no other name under heaven given among men by which we must be saved." (Acts 4:11-12)

If the people of Nineveh seemed to respond in self preservation, they only did so because they believed God and what He said. If they didn't think God had the power and authority to destroy them, they would have remained in pride rather than humbling themselves and turning to God. Like the sailors in the beginning of the story, they also had a healthy fear of God. They did not fear Jonah; they feared the message that came from the One they must fear. They could have easily overpowered Jonah, but they did not because they believed God's power and that God would not allow it.

GOD DEMONSTRATES MERCY

We see how Nineveh responded to Jonah and his message from God. At the end of Jonah 3 God responds.

> When God saw what they did, how they turned from their evil way, God relented of the disaster that he had said he would do to them, and he did not do it. (Jonah 3:10)

God's response was grace and mercy, He *"relented of the disaster."* God's message allowed for His mercy, giving them time to repent. It was a message of warning more than a promise. Nineveh responded in faith; first, they believed God, and as a result they humbled themselves and turned from their evil ways. God's message brought about repentance and a pouring out of His mercy on those who believed. Jesus spoke of this as it was written by Luke.

> The men of Nineveh will rise up at the judgment with this generation and condemn it, for they repented at the preaching of Jonah, and behold, something greater than Jonah is here. (Luke 11:32)

In our zeal for the Lord, we should desire mercy, even for the wicked. God extends grace to whom He chooses; it is not up to us to determine God's grace or mercy.

SUCCESS IN EVANGELISM

Nineveh's response was truly incredible. Jonah saw the salvation of a whole city, roughly half a million people, in less than 40 days. Is this what we desire for our nation or even our own hometown, much less for our enemies? A mass revival and turning toward God?

Most Christians affirm these desires but seek to accomplish them through earthly means or to measure them by earthly measures. Here is a simple example: After an event or evangelistic effort, people may ask, "How did it go?" They often anticipate answers such as: How many people accepted Christ? How many will show up at church on Sunday? How many people were baptized? If God is the one that makes them grow, and brings in the harvest, then these questions evaluate how God did rather than how we did in our labor. We should not question God's work, for His work cannot fail.

Other questions that might be useful when evaluating our impact might include these: How can I be more persuasive? Should I pray more? Was my heart in the right place, loving God and loving the lost? These are questions of wise counsel and can be helpful in our labor. However, they quickly fall apart when evaluating our evangelistic success because it is ultimately not our success at all, but God's.

God brought in a great harvest from the Ninevites. He accomplished that through the work of Jonah. That is why He sent him. I raise these key questions to evaluate your success in light of Jonah:

1. Was Jonah a better evangelist due to his skill, creativity, or experience in delivering the message?

2. Was he a more persuasive speaker, appealing to their needs?

3. Was his heart in the right place, loving the lost in Nineveh more or better than I?

4. Did he have a more compelling message for his audience?

5. Did the people of Nineveh elect a godly leader to lead them out of their evil and violence?

I hope the futility of these questions is evident. An evangelist is not a failure because he or she does not produce the numbers that Jonah did. Jonah didn't craft the message, it was God. Jonah was not more persuasive. His love of Nineveh was lackluster at best, and the King was just as guilty as the rest of Nineveh. It was not Jonah that made the revival successful, it was God. It was God's message; it was God who turned their hearts. Jonah was simply a reluctant, but eventually faithful servant. God worked through Jonah despite his weakness. Our job is to proclaim the truth. God produces the results. We should not claim His success as our own, but we should rejoice in it.

Just as with Jonah, God gives us the message—the Gospel. We have no need to tone it down to make it more acceptable, nor to sharpen it, hoping to drive more fear into the hearts of those who hear. We simply need to deliver it as God has given it, both the good news and the bad news. God's message is better and more effective than ours as His power for salvation.

> For I am not ashamed of the gospel, for it is the power of God for salvation to everyone who believes, to the Jew first and also to the Greek. (Romans 1:16)

Stick to the Gospel and you will be wielding the power of God to win souls. Evangelism is a labor, not a result. The gardener plants a garden, loosens the soil, digs a hole, and buries the seed. While waiting for the plants to emerge and grow, the gardener waters it, pulls up the weeds and helps provide the environment and nutrients needed for it to grow. But the gardener cannot force growth—only provide the input needed. It is God who creates the means and process for growth. A plant's growth is the sole responsibility of God. Likewise, the conversion of a soul is the work of the Holy Spirit. It is amazing to think that He uses us in this process, each with his own part. God brings this all together and makes it grow. Paul writes that each does his work as God has assigned, but God is responsible for the growth and harvest of that soul, not us.

> *For while there is jealousy and strife among you, are you not of the flesh and behaving only in a human way? For when one says, "I follow Paul," and another, "I follow Apollos," are you not being merely human? What then is Apollos? What is Paul? Servants through whom you believed, as the Lord assigned to each. I planted, Apollos watered, but God gave the growth. So neither he who plants nor he who waters is anything, but only God who gives the growth. (1 Corinthians 3:3-7)*

God prepares the hearts of men to receive the Gospel message through planting and watering. The harvest is His and we are His workers. We need to pray for more Christians to answer that call. We need to answer that call.

> *Then he said to his disciples, "The harvest is plentiful, but the laborers are few; therefore pray earnestly to the Lord of the harvest to send out laborers into his harvest." (Matthew 9:37-38)*

We labor to bring good news. The Gospel proclaims enmity between us and Him and gives a message of reconciliation to God through Christ; as it says, we are His ambassadors.

> *All this is from God, who through Christ reconciled us to himself and gave us the ministry of reconciliation; that is, in Christ God was reconciling the world to himself, not counting their trespasses against them, and entrusting to us the message of reconciliation. Therefore, we are ambassadors for Christ, God making his appeal through us. We implore you on behalf of Christ, be reconciled to God. (2 Corinthians 5:18-20)*

Do you see the Gospel in that passage? The message of reconciliation is that Christ died for our sins, *"not counting their trespasses against them."*

The message is unchanging; Christ died for our sin to reconcile us to Him. The message was the same in Jonah's time, but more fully revealed to us now in the New Testament. Just as the author of Hebrews says:

> *For good news came to us just as to them, but the message they heard did not benefit them, because they were not united by faith with those who listened. (Hebrews 4:2)*

The King James Version says this even more clearly:

> *For unto us was the gospel preached, as well as unto them (Hebrews 4:2)*

The Gospel is an aged message that has not changed–only clarified. It was effective then and is still effective today without a need for us to modernize the message to make it more relevant.

Let me propose some more relevant questions that will answer questions like *"How did it go?"*

1. Was a seed planted, or a plant watered with the Gospel?

2. Was Christ glorified and His name made known among men?

3. Did we bring someone to the foot of the cross to see their sin, and the atonement through Christ?

4. Was the Gospel message proclaimed, even if only partially?

Our success is in our faithfulness to labor in God's field. We may not know if we had an impact; we only see in part. We cannot judge the sincerity of another; only God knows the heart. We may not see a person ever again, but we trust God to carry through His work. We may not see the fruit of our labor until we arrive in heaven, but God will. He rewards the faithful servant.

How did Jonah do? He made the name of God known among the men of Nineveh and even the sailors on the ship to Tarshish. He proclaimed God's message to the whole of Nineveh. The message of God's judgment brought their knowledge of sin to the forefront, causing them to turn to God for their hope.

The growth and harvest belong to God, but if God grants us to see the response of even one person, we should rejoice as the angels do.

> *there will be more joy in heaven over one sinner who repents than over ninety-nine righteous persons who need no repentance. (Luke 15:7)*

Salvation belongs to the Lord! (Jonah 2:9)

8. JONAH DIALOGS WITH GOD

But it displeased Jonah exceedingly, and he was angry. (Jonah 4:1)

In the final chapter of Jonah, we return to Jonah behaving in the natural flesh. He is not fleeing, but he looks back, rationalizing his rebellion and trying to justify himself before God. Jonah was angry and he cried out in complaint to God. We cannot ignore how intensely he expressed this, yet God still did not abandon Jonah. He dealt with Jonah in patience, demonstrating His mercy. Every one of us, regardless of where we are in our journey of faith, need this kind of patience from God. We are often blinded by our earthly viewpoint or stuck in our own way of doing things. We need God to open our eyes to understand His perspective.

This dialog between Jonah and God is structured into three sections: The first four verses, Jonah prays to God and says, *I told you so*. In verses 5-9 God gives Jonah a physical illustration, prompting him to be more reflective. In the closing two verses God explains His motivation.

JONAH CRIES OUT IN ANGER AGAINST GOD

Jonah fulfilled his vow to follow God's command and bring His message to the people of Nineveh. He did it well, just as God had commanded, and did not hold back. Jonah had already suspected that God would not bring disaster on Nineveh and this made him angry.

> *And he prayed to the Lord and said, "O Lord, is not this what I said when I was yet in my country? That is why I made haste to flee to Tarshish; for I knew that you are a gracious God and merciful, slow to anger and abounding in steadfast love, and relenting from disaster. Therefore now, O Lord, please take my life from me, for it is better for me to die than to live." (Jonah 4:2-3)*

Even in his anger, he still honored God and turned to Him in prayer. He cried out, *"is not this what I said"* as he recalled his previous actions. He also praised God for His unequalled attributes of grace, mercy, patience, love, and compassion. Jonah cherished these attributes and desired them for himself, and for all of Israel, but he wrongfully desired disaster for Nineveh.

God's response to Jonah was full of grace and mercy. He could have reprimanded him harshly as He did when responding to Job.

> *Then the Lord answered Job out of the whirlwind and said: "Who is this that darkens counsel by words without knowledge? Dress for action like a man; I will question you, and you make it known to me. (Job 38:1-3)*

God responds to Jonah differently. God asked Jonah a question, prompting him to consider his words. The question implied that Jonah was wrong, without saying it outright.

> *And the Lord said, "Do you do well to be angry?" (Jonah 4:4)*

Remember the story of Cain and Abel in Genesis? God spoke kindly to Cain, pointing him to his sin. It was a gentle warning to repent and not be mastered by his sin.

> *The Lord said to Cain, "Why are you angry, and why has your face fallen? If you do well, will you not be accepted? And if you do not do well, sin is crouching at the door. Its desire is contrary to you, but you must rule over it." (Genesis 4:6-7)*

Jonah's anger was wrong, but God's mercy was greater.

GOD REVEALS HIMSELF TO JONAH

In the next section, God used things in the physical world to help Jonah see his situation more objectively. First, Jonah built himself a shelter, probably with branches as a roof to block the heat of the sun. He revealed his desire to see Nineveh destroyed while he attempted to sit in comfort.

> *Jonah went out of the city and sat to the east of the city and made a booth for himself there. He sat under it in the shade, till he should see what would become of the city. (Jonah 4:5)*

Jonah had completed his vow faithfully and completely. He went through the entire city of Nineveh proclaiming its destruction, just as God commanded. Geographically, Jonah came from the west and now emerged east of the city.

However, the shelter he built was not enough: he was not in comfort.

> *Now the Lord God appointed a plant and made it come up over Jonah, that it might be a shade over his head, to save him from his discomfort. So Jonah was exceedingly glad because of the plant. But when dawn came up the next day, God appointed a worm that attacked the plant, so that it withered. When the sun rose, God appointed a scorching east wind, and the sun beat down on the head of Jonah so that he was faint. And he asked that he might die and said, "It is better for me to die than to live." (Jonah 4:4-8)*

God revealed Himself to Jonah through His sovereignty over all His creation. God appointed a plant, and it obeyed. The plant provided the shade Jonah needed; he was glad. His comfort only lasted a day as God appointed a worm to destroy it. He added more pressure to Jonah through the wind and sun to emphasize His point. Did God desire his discomfort and suffering?

Allow me to paint this picture a little more. The plant that God sent is translated from the Hebrew word, "kikayon." It is a fast-growing plant with very large leaves over a foot in breadth. Some translate this word as a vine or gourd, which also fits the description. Many believe it to be the *Ricinus communis*, or castor oil plant. It grows quickly, up to 8-10 feet tall, and withers away just as rapidly. [1]

Most Americans live with the benefit of air conditioning and shelter for both work and home. I once visited India for my job; it was around 110 degrees Fahrenheit for two weeks straight. The office and hotel were air-conditioned, but one Saturday we visited the Taj Mahal in Agra. We spent most of the day outside enjoying the attraction. By the end of the day after several hours in the

---

1. https://en.wikipedia.org/wiki/Kikayon

heat of the sun, all I wanted to do was to sit in the shade to get some relief. I can understand how Jonah was faint.

In this short physical illustration, we can see a small reflection of the Gospel. God provided the plant to give Jonah some shade, as it says, *"to save him."* A Christian finds great comfort in the salvation that God provides, but we often try to save ourselves. Jonah tried to provide shade for himself but his efforts building the booth for shade were not enough. It is God who provided salvation; nothing we do can compare. In fact, without God and His work, we remain in misery and are destined for more.

Jonah held to his own perspective and remained in anger despite the relief he had received from God. God responded again with patience and mercy, while Jonah became more stubborn.

> But God said to Jonah, "Do you do well to be angry for the plant?" And he said, "Yes, I do well to be angry, angry enough to die." (Jonah 4:9)

THE CONCLUSION OF THEIR DIALOG

God speaks and reveals Jonah's blindness. God chastises Jonah.

> And the Lord said, "You pity the plant, for which you did not labor, nor did you make it grow, which came into being in a night and perished in a night. (Jonah 4:10)

Likewise, David was blinded by his sin with Bathsheba until God sent the prophet Nathan to reveal it to him through a simple story (2 Samuel 12:1-13).

Jonah's salvation was not his own doing, it was from God. The writings of the Apostles in the New Testament provide us with the same theme.

> For by grace you have been saved through faith. And this is not your own doing; it is the gift of God, not a result of works, so that no one may boast. (Ephesians 2:8-9)

Jonah's anger should have turned to thankfulness as it did when he prayed from the belly of the great fish.

In the final verse, God explains His motivation for relenting from disaster and saving the people of Nineveh. He appeals to Jonah's conscience and asks Jonah:

> And should not I pity Nineveh, that great city, in which there are more than 120,000 persons who do not know their right hand from their left, and also much cattle?" (Jonah 4:11)

We are told that 120,000 people lived in Nineveh, probably more. Nineveh was a great city, one of the largest of its time. It was likely a growing city due to its military strength and conquest of the surrounding nations. Even a population of 120,000 people was considered large at that time. Nineveh was an old and established city; it was built roughly 2000 years before Jonah. It is recorded in Genesis that Nimrod, the great grandson of Noah, built it only a few generations after the great flood.

> *Cush fathered Nimrod; he was the first on earth to be a mighty man. He was a mighty hunter before the Lord. Therefore it is said, "Like Nimrod a mighty hunter before the Lord." The beginning of his kingdom was Babel, Erech, Accad, and Calneh, in the land of Shinar. From that land he went into Assyria and built Nineveh, Rehoboth-Ir, Calah, and Resen between Nineveh and Calah; that is the great city. (Genesis 10:8-12)*

The rhetorical question has an obvious answer: Yes, God should have pity for that great city. God reveals His motive and concern for the *"least of these."* His compassion for them was foreshadowed in the opening verses of Jonah where God sends Jonah to *"call out against it, for their evil has come up before me."*

When Jesus speaks of the coming judgment and separating the sheep from the goats, His compassion is evident. We are called to love and show compassion for our neighbors.

> *'Truly, I say to you, as you did it to one of the least of these my brothers, you did it to me.' (Matthew 25:40)*

Even amid His own proclamation of the Gospel, Jesus speaks of His compassion for the lost.

> *And Jesus went throughout all the cities and villages, teaching in their synagogues and proclaiming the gospel of the kingdom and healing every disease and every affliction. When he saw the crowds, he had compassion for them, because they were harassed and helpless, like sheep without a shepherd. Then he said to his disciples, "The harvest is plentiful, but the laborers are few; therefore pray earnestly to the Lord of the harvest to send out laborers into his harvest." (Matthew 9:35-38)*

As we proclaim the Gospel, or share Christ with our neighbor, our effort and our speech should be saturated with compassion for them and love for Christ.

The population of the city of Nineveh was at least 120,000 people; it may have been larger. This verse counts those *"who do not know their right hand from their left."* Some interpret this as those who were spiritually illiterate or ignorant, implying the whole population of Nineveh was in view. Others understand this to mean those who were too young to understand, literally not knowing their right from left. If this is the meaning, then the population was over half a million people. With either interpretation, it is amazing to think that God turned the entire population of this ancient city to Himself through a message spoken by one man, filled with the Word of God.

In everyday life, we shape our own view of what is right. We want to protect ourselves and those we love, which can put us at odds with others—even our neighbors. It is good to defend the weak and the powerless, but God calls us to an even higher standard: to love our enemies. God demonstrated His compassion and showed us that the most loving thing we can do for them is to share His message. He can change them where we cannot.

9. THE REST OF
THE STORY

And being found in human form, he humbled himself by becoming obedient to the point of death, even death on a cross. Therefore God has highly exalted him and bestowed on him the name that is above every name, so that at the name of Jesus every knee should bow, in heaven and on earth and under the earth, and every tongue confess that Jesus Christ is Lord, to the glory of God the Father. (Philippians 2:8-11)

Do you see Christ more clearly when reading Jonah? Do you see His Gospel message in the text? More importantly, do you see God and His work through history? There is much more to this story, and I encourage you to discover more.

Throughout the whole Bible, God is always the main character! When we read Jonah, we are drawn to him or to Nineveh as our focus, but they are secondary. Instead, we must ask the question: What do we learn about God through the ways He interacts with men, both the righteous and the wicked? The Bible is God's story, just as the Gospel is God's message.

God's story of salvation is unfolding for us in His Word and in the world around us. It is real, not myth. It is a struggle we are all engaged in that began with the deception of man in the Garden of Eden, bringing in pain, suffering, and ultimately death because of Adam's sin. As the struggle begins, God gives us a vision of hope and victory, found only in the death of His son.

> *I will put enmity between you and the woman, and between your offspring and her off-spring; he shall bruise your head, and you shall bruise his heel." (Genesis 3:15)*

Jonah was in this struggle pursuing his desire to just live his life by fleeing from God and His command. In God's overwhelming love and compassion, He does not allow Jonah's flight but pursues Jonah on the sea for His purpose. Today, Christ compels us by the Great Commission to bring the Gospel to everyone.

Nineveh was in this struggle, pursuing self and their own desires, relying on their human strength, and their penchant for violence. God awakens them from their blindness by His message delivered through Jonah. In God's mercy, He turns their hearts to Him and abandons their destruction.

It is a struggle that ends with faith—only in Christ.

WHAT ABOUT NINEVEH?

Israel was in this struggle throughout their history in the Bible. Israel was constantly in conflict with Assyria which was represented as the wicked, lawless enemy of God. But in this incredible demonstration of God's love this generation was saved. Then, roughly 40 years later the next generation of Ninevites returned to their former evil ways and took Israel captive.

> *In the ninth year of Hoshea, the king of Assyria captured Samaria, and he carried the Is-raelites away to Assyria and placed them in Halah, and on the Habor, the river of Gozan, and in the cities of the Medes. (2 Kings 17:6)*

God raised up Assyria to discipline Israel because of their disobedience.

> *And this occurred because the people of Israel had sinned against the Lord their God, who had brought them up out of the land of Egypt from under the hand of Pharaoh king of Egypt, and had feared other gods and walked in the customs of the nations whom the Lord drove out before the people of Israel, and in the customs that the kings of Israel had practiced. (2 Kings 17:7-8)*

Assyria was not innocent but served God's purpose; He punished them by sending lions.

NIMROD BUILDS NINEVEH		*JONAH PROPHESIES*	*NINEVEH DESTROYED*
23rd Century B.C.		*760 B.C.*	*612 B.C.*
	ASSYRIAN EMPIRE RISES		*ASSYRIA CAPTURES SAMARIA*
	13th Century B.C.		*722 B.C.*

Christ is born

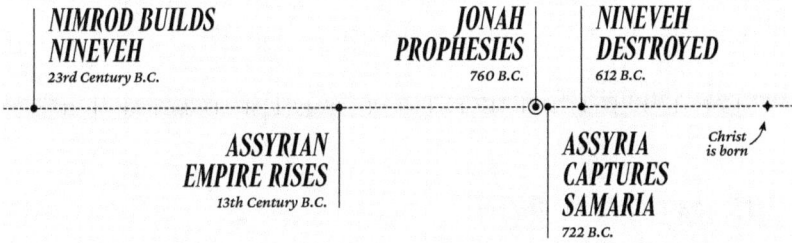

Nineveh had a long history before Jonah, beginning shortly after the global flood.

> *And at the beginning of their dwelling there, they did not fear the Lord. Therefore the Lord sent lions among them, which killed some of them. (2 Kings 17:25)*

The people of Assyria continued in rebellion against God and the result was complete destruction only 150 years after Jonah's visit. The prophets Nahum and Isaiah foretold Assyria's destruction, and history confirms that Assyria was destroyed in 612 B.C.

Jonah struggled against bringing a message of hope to God's enemies. He was disciplined and restored by God but not destroyed. God redeemed the people of Nineveh at that time but later destroyed their nation in His timing and for His purpose. Eventually, all of God's enemies will be destroyed.

Even today with a growing decline in morality, we are reminded of God's patience and mercy and His promise to rescue us *"from this present evil age"* (Galatians 1:4). We can identify with Lot who was surrounded by lawlessness. Peter writes about the destruction of Sodom and Gomorrah as a demonstration of God's power to rescue the godly and punish the ungodly.

> *if by turning the cities of Sodom and Gomorrah to ashes he condemned them to extinction, making them an example of what is going to happen to the ungodly; and if he rescued righteous Lot, greatly distressed by the sensual conduct of the wicked (for as that righteous man lived among them day after day, he was tormenting his righteous soul over their lawless deeds that he saw and heard); then the Lord knows how to rescue the godly from trials, and to keep the unrighteous under punishment until the day of judgment. (2 Peter 2:6-9)*

Christians can identify with Lot as he was surrounded by the increasing wickedness. Jonah surely faced fear as he walked into Nineveh, surrounded by those who hated him and the One he represented. We may not always understand His ways, but this is where God has placed us in His plan.

God builds up and God destroys.

THE BATTLE IS WON

We still live out this struggle today, knowing that the battle has been won by Christ and His shed blood. His death means we are no longer under God's wrath and will not be condemned when He returns. We wait for a time when Christ returns and restores all things, removing the effects of sin and sending the wicked away to their eternal punishment.

Jonah's hope was rooted in the Messiah that God had promised through the prophets. There was still much that was unknown to Jonah, yet he had faith. Jonah may not have known how his life foreshadowed the Messiah, but God did. We have the teaching of the Apostles who saw Christ face to face.

Our knowledge of the Messiah has increased with the advent of Christ. Numerous prophecies have come to fruition; not all are yet realized. The mystery of the Messiah has decreased but will be completely fulfilled with His return.

Our faith is not blind but is based on a confidence in God who has always been faithful and will bring about all of His promises: a God who even the wind and the seas obey, a God who turned the hearts of the great city of Nineveh, a God who is still alive and in authority today and will bring about His purposes according to His timing. The prophecies that are not yet fulfilled will be fulfilled when He returns.

GOD'S PLAN OF SALVATION

At the beginning of this book, I quoted Acts 3:24 saying that *all the prophets proclaimed these days* of Christ. Here I provide further context for this passage. As you read it, I hope it brings back memories of the events of Jonah's story.

> *But what God foretold by the mouth of all the prophets, that his Christ would suffer, he thus fulfilled. Repent therefore, and turn back, that your sins may be blotted out, that times of refreshing may come from the presence of the Lord, and that he may send the*

Christ appointed for you, Jesus, whom heaven must receive until the time for restoring all the things about which God spoke by the mouth of his holy prophets long ago. Moses said, 'The Lord God will raise up for you a prophet like me from your brothers. You shall listen to him in whatever he tells you. And it shall be that every soul who does not listen to that prophet shall be destroyed from the people.' And all the prophets who have spoken, from Samuel and those who came after him, also proclaimed these days. You are the sons of the prophets and of the covenant that God made with your fathers, saying to Abraham, 'And in your offspring shall all the families of the earth be blessed.' (Acts 3:18-25)

In the story of Jonah:

— Salvation is from the Lord, not through the works of man.

— Neither Jonah nor Nineveh were worthy of God's salvation.

— Those who listened to God's message were saved from destruction.

— If they would not have listened, God would have destroyed them as He promised.

— They were saved by grace through faith and God transformed them and made them new.

God is fulfilling His promise to Abraham to bless all nations, even extending salvation to the Gentiles. He extended salvation to Nineveh and He extends it to us.

I will surely bless you, and I will surely multiply your offspring as the stars of heaven and as the sand that is on the seashore. And your offspring shall possess the gate of his enemies, and in your offspring shall all the nations of the earth be blessed, because you have obeyed my voice." (Genesis 22:17-18)

There is no greater news than this! God saves the undeserving.

For while we were still weak, at the right time Christ died for the ungodly. (Romans 5:6)

WE ANXIOUSLY AWAIT THE RETURN OF CHRIST

The Bible urges us to be prepared, not idle, while we wait.

Now we command you, brothers, in the name of our Lord Jesus Christ, that you keep away from any brother who is walking in idleness and not in accord with the tradition that you received from us. (2 Thessalonians 3:6)

We find the same encouragement through Jesus' two parables prior to the announcement of final judgment in Matthew 25. The parables of the Ten Virgins (verses 1-13) and the Ten Talents (verses 14-31) teach us to actively be ready, prepare, and use what God has given as a faithful servant advancing the cause of his master. Matthew concludes this chapter with an illustration of Christ at the final judgment, separating the sheep from the goats.

Peter urges us to be prepared, and that starts by honoring Christ as holy. Christ is first and stands alone with no equals.

> *but in your hearts honor Christ the Lord as holy, always being prepared to make a defense to anyone who asks you for a reason for the hope that is in you; yet do it with gentleness and respect, (1 Peter 3:15)*

Most Christians agree, our hope is in Christ; we fix our eyes upon Him. Yet, in our daily walk, our actions may reflect a different view. Some seem to build their hope in government and politics, striving to elect the right people or to enact the right laws. The king of Nineveh was not the right person to reform the nation from a human perspective, but He was the right one in God's plan. Some seem to place their hope in the goodness and kindness of mankind; yet men fail. Some pursue diversity, creating a culture of inclusion. Tolerance of other god's only allows a veneer of peace with no true future hope. There is only one God and one truth. These pursuits can be noble and right but will not save and transform a people or culture like the Gospel can.

Only Christ can save, He has given us the Gospel. The core of the Gospel is the death, burial, and resurrection of Christ for the atonement of our sin. It is only through Him that we are reconciled to God and saved from God's wrath and eternal punishment. The Gospel is God's prescribed message to save mankind (Romans 1:16). Do not lean on man's wisdom, or our own persuasiveness, but upon God's message: the Gospel.

Our hope is in Christ; all other means will fail.

WHAT CAN WE DO?

What can we do now, how can we stem the tide of wickedness in our culture? How can we protect ourselves and others from a lawless and violent culture?

First, we can live lives that follow the wisdom found in God's word. Jeremiah gave Israel the same direction as they lived captive in Babylon (Jeremiah 29:4-9). In other words, do not conform to the patterns of this world and follow the culture (Romans 12:2), but follow God. Live a life that advances the Kingdom within you and your family and all that is in your control.

Second, be faithful to the Great Commission given by Jesus before He ascended. Share the Gospel! Use words to explain what Christ has done and give those around you a hope that they cannot accomplish themselves. Prepare them to be transformed by God.

Our hope is in God; it is in the Gospel message that turns hearts away from wickedness. Our hope is not in man: not in laws we make, not in the things we do, not in rulers we elect, not in the right education, but only in Christ. There is no other name which can save but Jesus.

Jesus is victorious; He conquered death and hades, and when He returns every knee will bow and every tongue will confess Jesus as Lord (Philippians 2:10-11). We will bow either as a servant of the King, or as a conquered rebel.

HOW DO WE EVALUATE JONAH AND HIS ROLE?

Jonah's reputation among Christians is often negative. He is characterized by his failings rather than his faithfulness. Should he be? King David broke many of God's commandments while pursuing Bathsheba. His son, King Solomon, had 700 wives and concubines. Paul killed many Christians, even overseeing and approving the stoning of Stephen. Moses angered God enough that he was prevented from entering the promised land. Yet, we expect to see every one of them in heaven. I expect to see Jonah.

Among the Jews, Jonah is honored as a true prophet. There were many false prophets who have now received their just punishment, but few true prophets. A true prophet is honored as he speaks the true word of the living God. Jesus commended Jonah.

> *The men of Nineveh will rise up at the judgment with this generation and condemn it, for they repented at the preaching of Jonah, and behold, something greater than Jonah is here. (Matthew 12:41)*

The Bible holds no one in moral perfection, except for Christ. Jonah was faithful in preaching God's message to the Ninevites and carrying out His command. God used Jonah to accomplish His purpose, despite his flaws and shortcomings.

Arise, Go! Preach the Gospel and make Christ known in your community and in our nation.

God will use you, in your weakness, until He returns.

APPENDIX

GRACE, MERCY, AND JUSTICE

Grace and mercy are common words among Christian authors and audiences. It can be difficult to distinguish between grace and mercy since these words are often used interchangeably. Both words can be understood in the context of justice. I sought to use these words consistently in my writing and in a way that is aligned with the Biblical context of the passage in which it is used.

Grace is the unmerited favor of God.

The primary definition of grace is the unmerited, or undeserved, favor of God, especially as it applies to the Gospel and our salvation. God gave us a gift that we do not deserve–eternal life with Him. In a system of justice, grace implies our guilt and the consequences for the crime that was committed. Because of our rebellion against God (sin), we deserve death, even eternal death.

> *For the wages of sin is death, but the free gift of God is eternal life in Christ Jesus our Lord. (Romans 6:23)*

In our guilt, justice and judgment are synonymous; God cannot give us what we deserve without giving us judgment. It is God's grace that gives us eternal life. This is the grace that saves.

Grace has other definitions: it can mean an act of kindness, or a temporary exemption such as a grace period, or even our prayer seeking God's grace.

Grace may also refer to a pleasing appearance or movement as one may walk or dance with grace.

The Roman Catholic Church defines grace differently; they include the "unmerited divine assistance given to humans for their regeneration or sanctification". This definition changes the good news of salvation from a gift to an accomplishment with God's aid. Salvation is from the Lord, not from our works. Using this definition turns the Gospel upside down: from an accomplishment of Christ on the cross, to an accomplishment of man, earning merit through their works, spurred on by God. This type of grace does enable the Christian in our daily lives, but it does not earn our salvation. Salvation, and its many aspects, is completely an undeserved gift from God.

Mercy is compassionate treatment of an offender.

The clearest expression of mercy in the story of Jonah is displayed in God's compassion (Jonah 4:11), relenting from the promise of disaster (Jonah 3:10). Grace and mercy can be understood as opposite sides of the same coin. What Jonah deserved for his rebellion was death, but God relented (mercy) and appointed a great fish to save him (grace). Likewise, it is an act of mercy for a Christian to warn an unbeliever, like warning a blind man of the danger ahead as he walks toward a cliff. Mercy, in the context of justice, also implies guilt and removes the consequence from the offender.

Justice is conformity to God's standard of what is morally good and to receive what is fair and reasonable.

For every action there is a just consequence: when you touch a hot stove you will get burned, when you commit a crime there is punishment, and when you act rightly you receive recognition or satisfaction, when you pay for a product, you receive it. On the contrary, if you pay for a product and don't receive it or if it does not function as advertised, that is injustice.

Justice is conformity to truth, fact, and reason. A judge seeks to bring about justice by hearing the case, listening to witnesses, and evaluating the situation with reason. On earth, justice is incomplete because of man's imperfection; it may also be perverted because of man's corruption. Man's knowledge and wisdom is incomplete, but God's is not. God is all-knowing and all-wise. Nothing is hidden from God; only He can bring about true justice in every situation. He also has the power and authority to ensure the judgment is carried to completion, though it may be delayed compared to our expectations.

> Beloved, never avenge yourselves, but leave it to the wrath of God, for it is written, "Vengeance is mine, I will repay, says the Lord." (Romans 12:19)

God is full of grace, mercy, and justice; these three are bound together in His love. Mankind sins and rebels against God, earning death as Jonah and Nineveh did. God does not merely sweep our offense under the rug; that would make Him an unjust Judge. Our crime must be punished, and it will be. In His love for us, He fulfills justice by sending His Son Jesus to pay what we owe. When Christ returns to judge the world, every person who ever lived will either receive justice (eternal death for their sin) or they will receive grace because of God's love and their faith in Christ.

AND ALSO MUCH CATTLE

And should not I pity Nineveh, that great city, in which there are more than 120,000 persons who do not know their right hand from their left, and also much cattle?" (Jonah 4:11)

Will there be animals in heaven?

This question is prompted by the closing verse of Jonah, *"and also much cattle."* The king's proclamation to humble themselves before God included the animals and God demonstrates His concern for the animals in this closing verse.

Animals are a part of God's very good creation

We read in Genesis 1 that God created animals and called them *good*, creating each *kind* on day five (Genesis 1:20-23) and day six (Genesis 1:24-25). God gave them the command to *"be fruitful and multiply"*; He desired them to fill the earth. It makes sense that God would include animals in the afterlife, as He will remove the effects of the curse of sin and restores all things. Isaiah describes this in a familiar passage, declaring, *"the wolf shall dwell with the lamb."* (Isaiah 11:6-9)

God demonstrates His love and value of animals

Consider these passages that show us how God provides for the animals:

— The young lions roar for their prey, seeking their food from God (Psalm 104:21).

— He gives the beasts their food, and to the young ravens that cry (Psalm 147:9).

— Man and beast you save, O Lord (Psalm 36:6).

— He will tend his flock like a shepherd; He will gather the lambs in His arms (Isaiah 40:11).

— Ask the beasts, and they will teach you... Who among all these does not know that the hand of the Lord has done this (Job 12:7-10)?

— Are not five sparrows sold for two pennies? And not one of them is forgotten before God (Luke 12:6).

— Look at the birds of the air: they neither sow nor reap nor gather into barns, and yet your heavenly Father feeds them (Matthew 6:26).

God saved each *kind* of animal in the ark when He sent the flood of Noah's day (Genesis 6:19-20), preserving their ability to re-populate the earth. He challenged Jonah with His compassion for the people of Nineveh *and also much cattle* (Jonah 4:11).

God also uses animals to describe His attributes such as a hen protecting her chicks (Luke 13:34). Even more, God uses animals as names to refer to Christ, His beloved Son. Christ is the *Lamb of God*, who takes away the sin of the world (John 1:29), and He is the *Lion of the Tribe of Judah* (Revelation 5:5).

God created man in His image

On day six, after creating the animals, God created mankind in Adam (Genesis 1:26-27). He declared that man was created in His own image and holds a special place of love and value. Man and animal are separate created *kinds*, not evolved from the same ancestor but designed by God. He commanded man to *subdue the earth* and *have dominion* over the animals (Genesis 1:28).

Man was created to have a bond with animals, but not as equals. In Genesis 2, God brought each animal kind to Adam to name them. After Adam finished naming them, God set apart man by saying none were *fit for Adam, so* God created Eve.

God gave purpose for man and animals, each one is different, according to its kind. Each is designed for God's purpose and His glory. Man's rule over the animals is governed by expectations; we are to care for them as God would. We are His steward, not owners without accountability. We are given right and wrong ways to care for and govern the animals. Consider these verses:

— You shall not muzzle an ox when it is treading out the grain (Deuteronomy 25:4).

— If you see the donkey of one who hates you lying down under its burden, you shall refrain from leaving him with it; you shall rescue it with him (Exodus 23:5).

— On the seventh day you shall rest; that your ox and your donkey may have rest (Exodus 23:12).

— Let the feet of the ox and the donkey range free (Isaiah 32:20).

— When an ox or sheep or goat is born, it shall remain seven days with its mother (Leviticus 22:27).

— Which of you, having a son or an ox that has fallen into a well on a Sabbath day, will not immediately pull him out? (Luke 14:5)

— Know well the condition of your flocks and give attention to your herds (Proverbs 27:23).

— Whoever is righteous has regard for the life of his beast, but the mercy of the wicked is cruel (Proverbs 12:10).

God has blessed them all.

Jesus said, "*Consider the lilies... even Solomon was not arrayed like one of these... how much more will he clothe you.*" (Luke 12:27-28) He also said, "*Fear not, therefore; you are of more value than many sparrows.*" (Matthew 10:31)

TulipGospelOutreach.org

To mobilize Christians to publicly share the gospel with unbelievers in their local community. This will be done through education, imitation, and opportunity.

— **Education**: providing information and Biblical principles to equip the believer and build confidence to labor for the harvest. (Ephesians 4:11-13)

— **Imitation**: providing mentors and experience to develop and encourage Christian evangelists in this work. (1 Corinthians 11:1)

— **Opportunity**: providing local group opportunities and resources to put the Great Commission into practice. (Matthew 28:18-20)

www.ingramcontent.com/pod-product-compliance
Lightning Source LLC
LaVergne TN
LVHW021409080426
835508LV00020B/2520